HOUSE OF HORRORS
MONSTER MAZE COLORING BOOK

Illustrated by
Tyler Rea

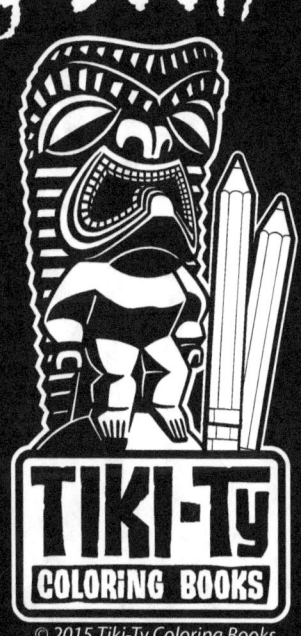

TIKI-Ty COLORING BOOKS

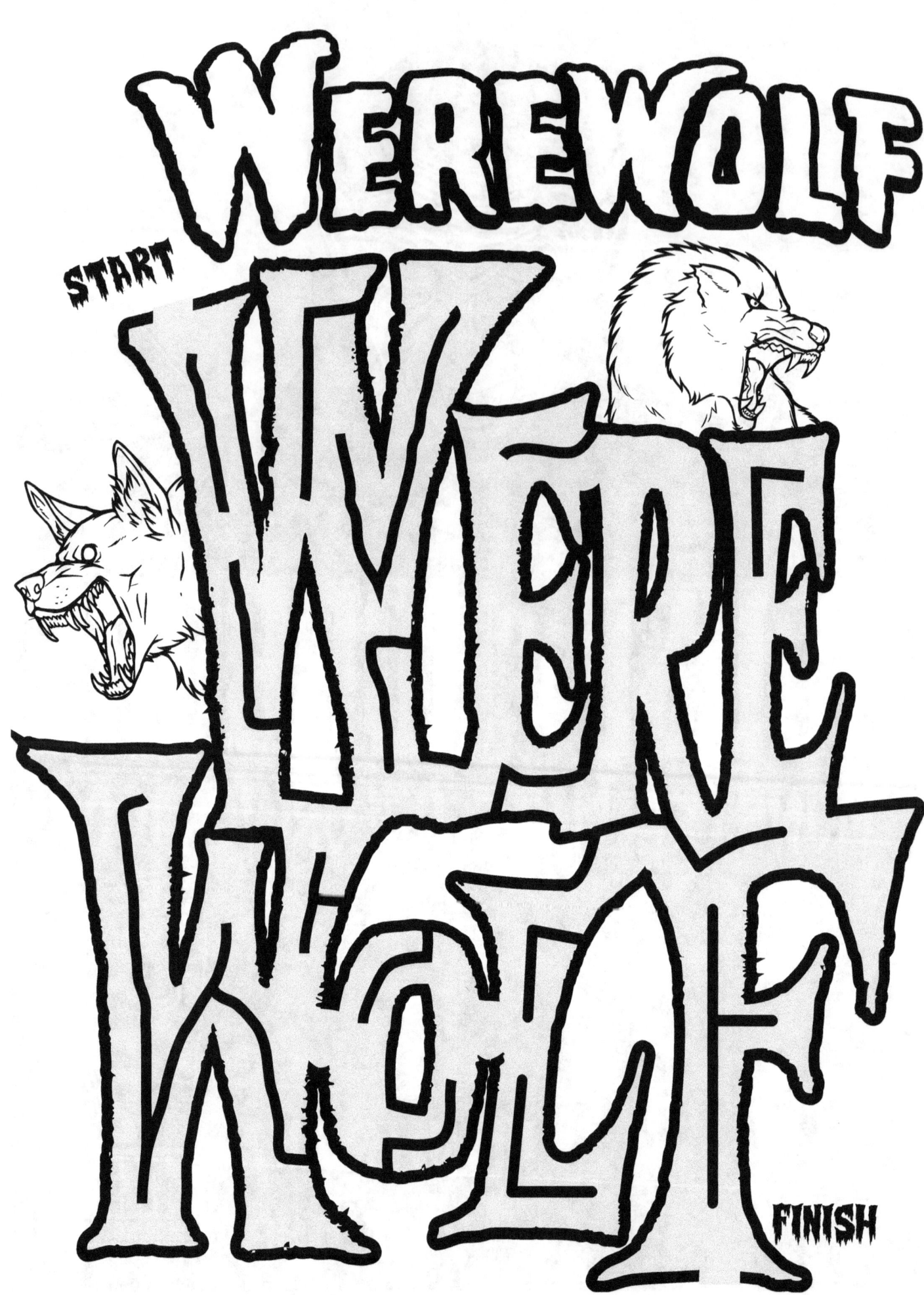

START

GHOST

FINISH

RiP

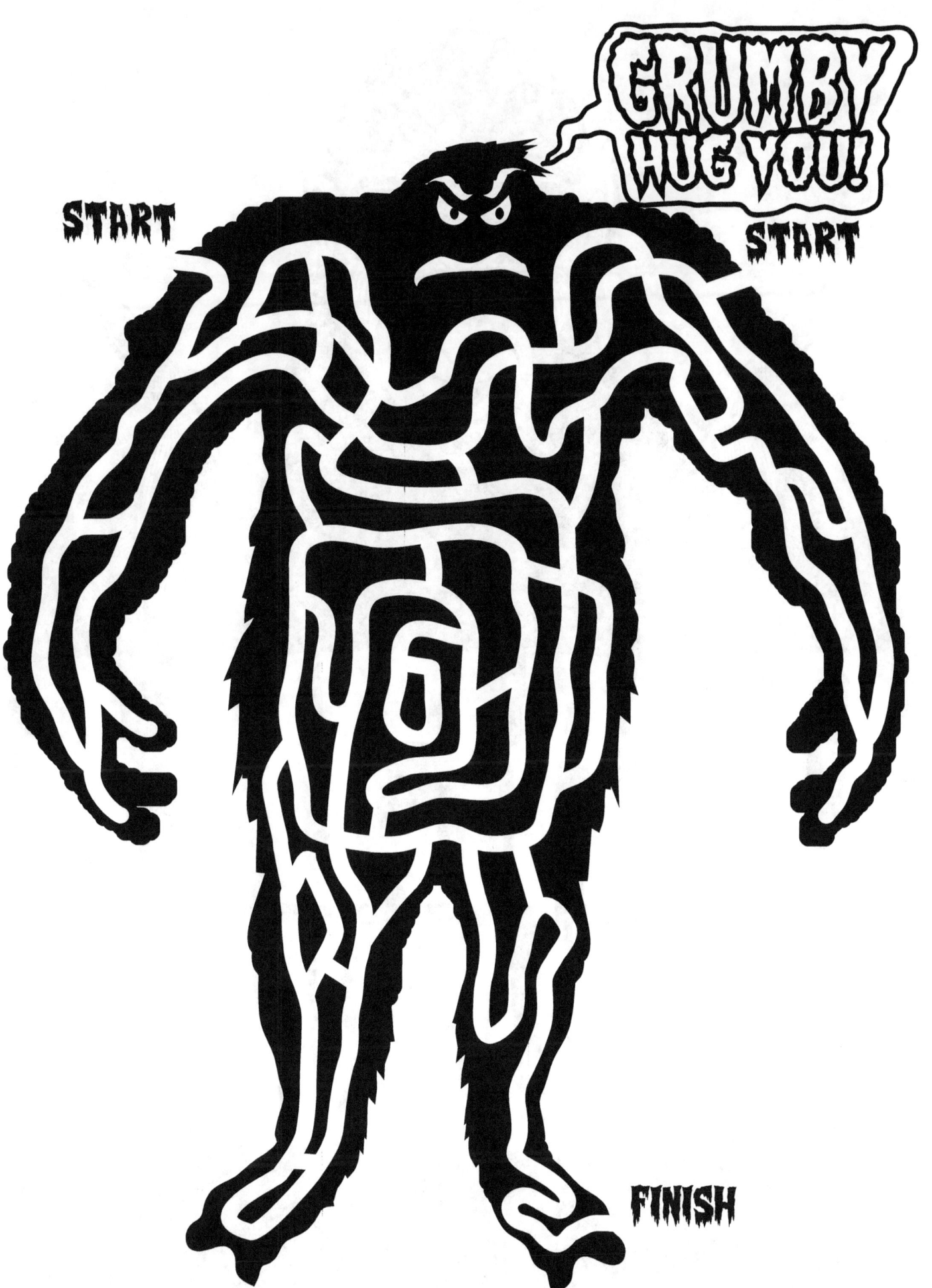

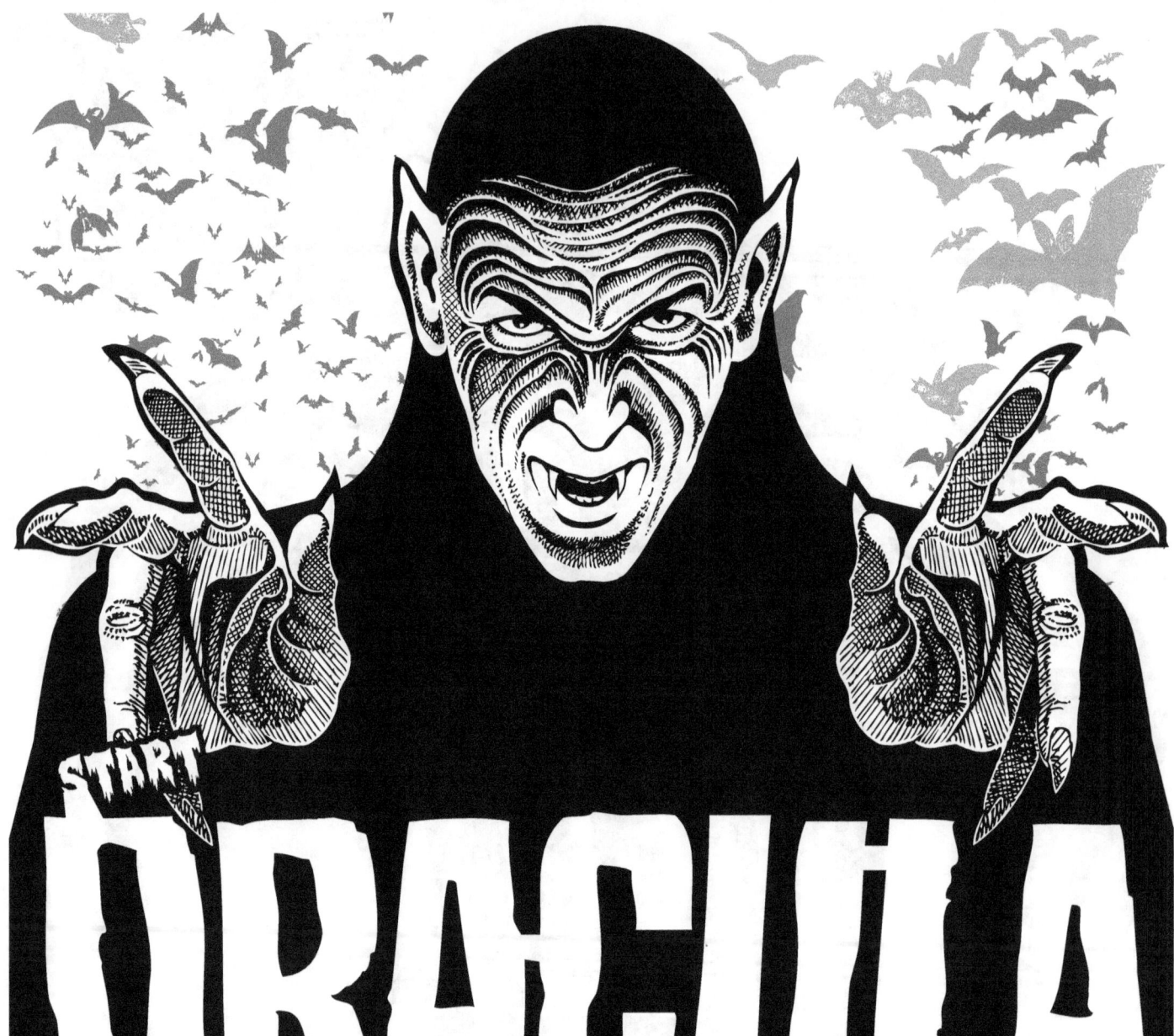

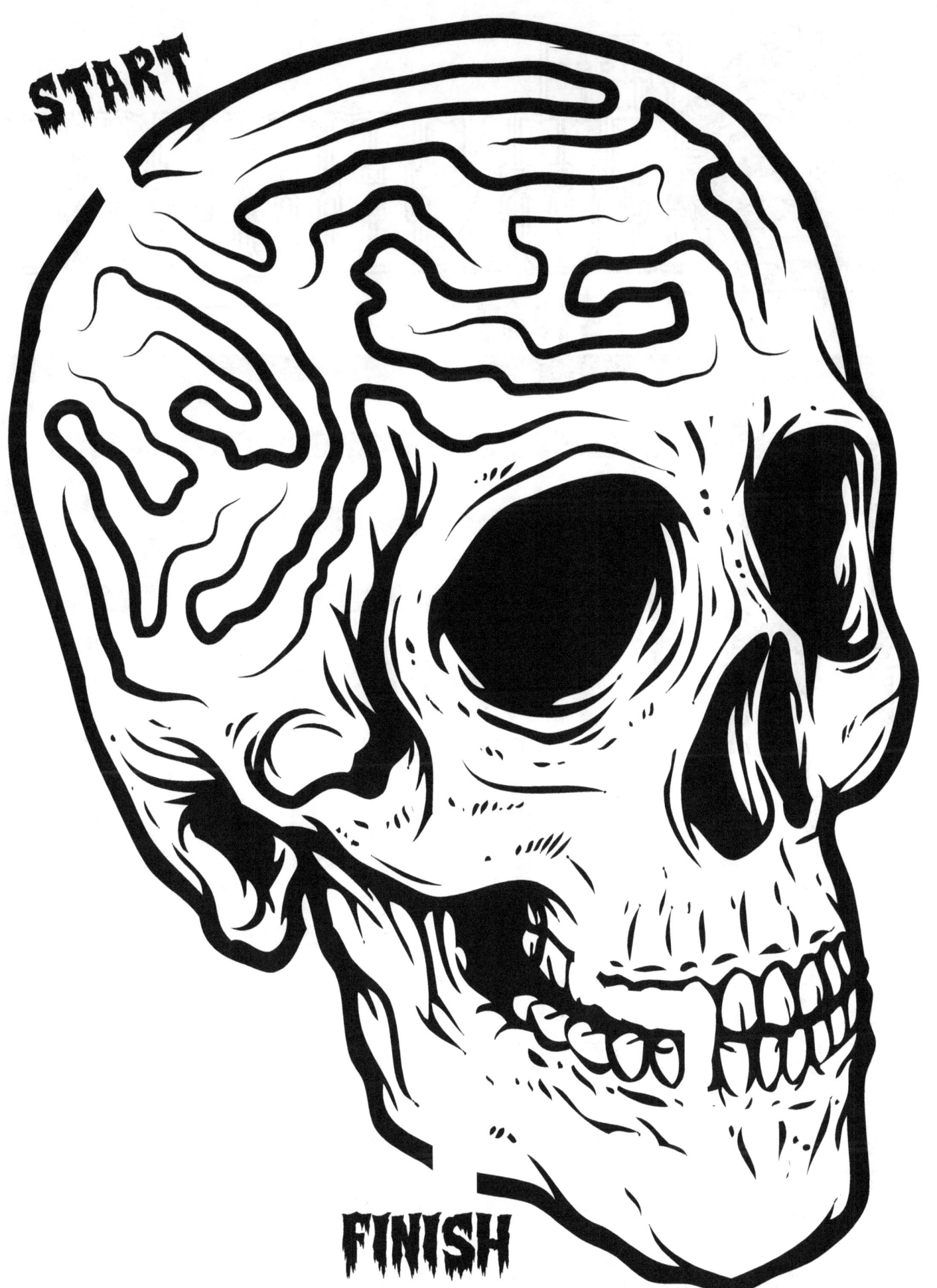

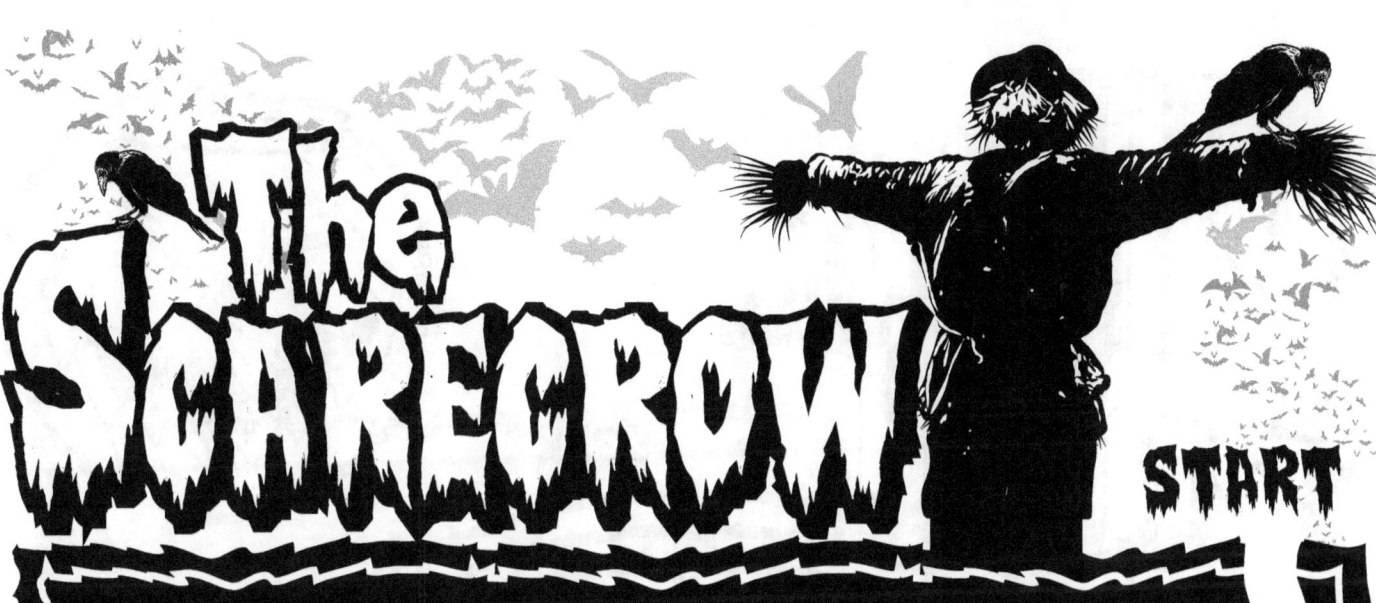

START

FINISH

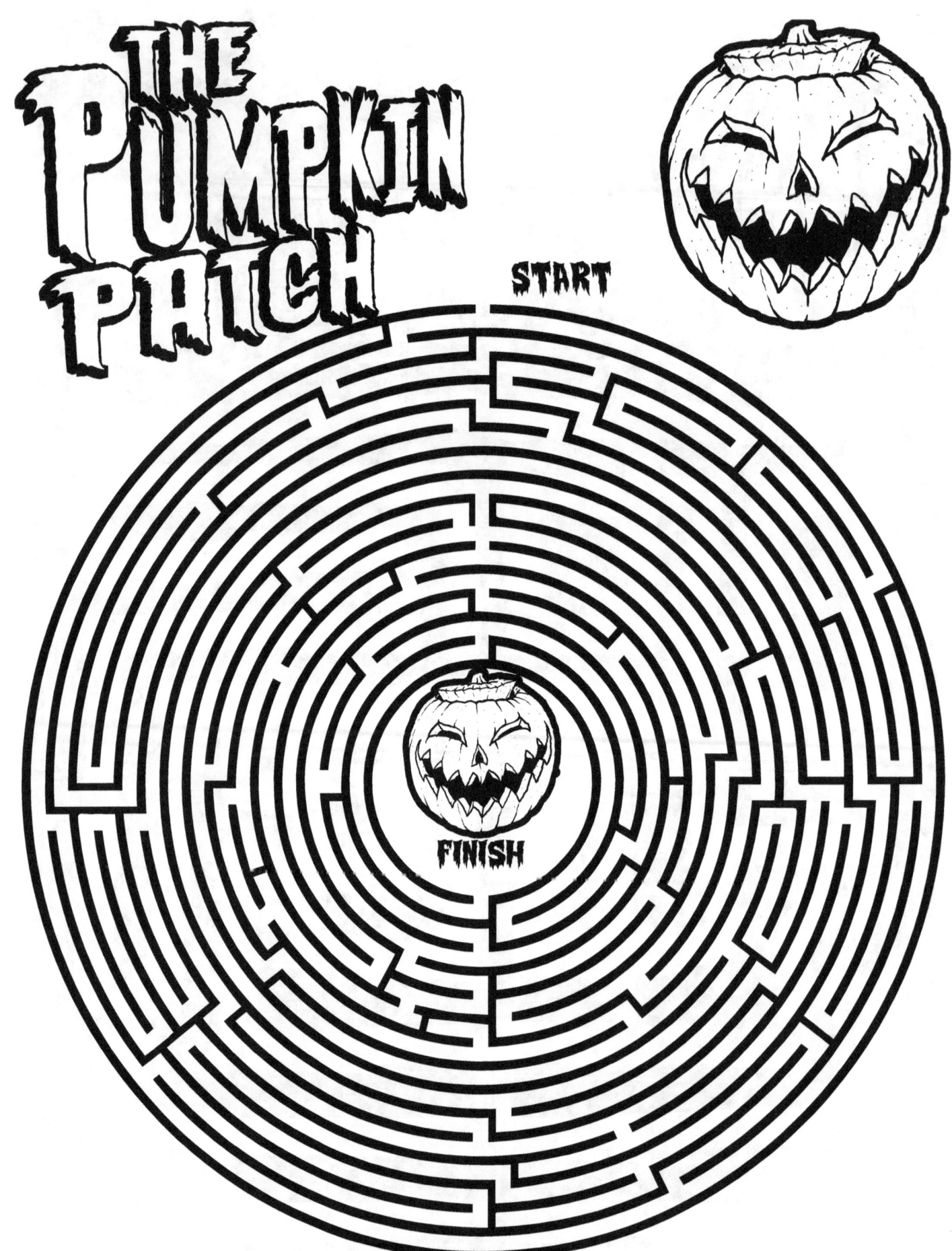

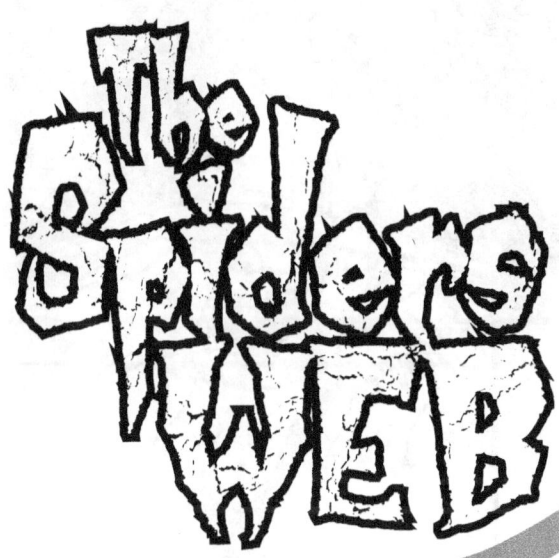

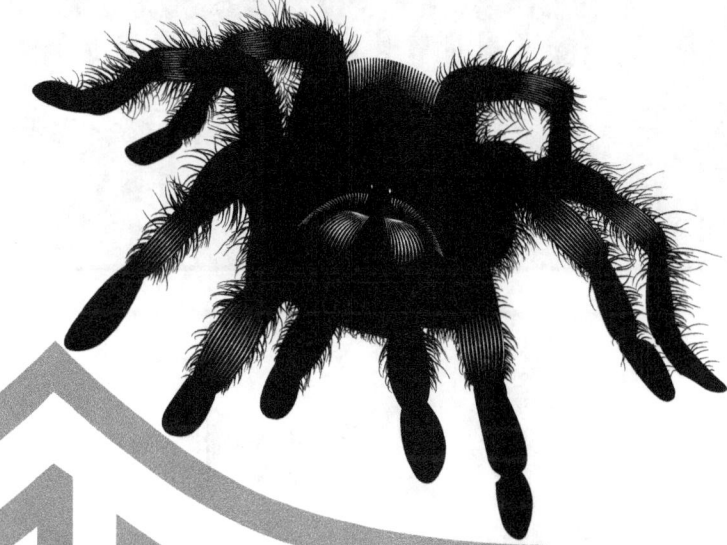

START

FINISH

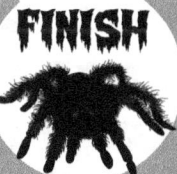

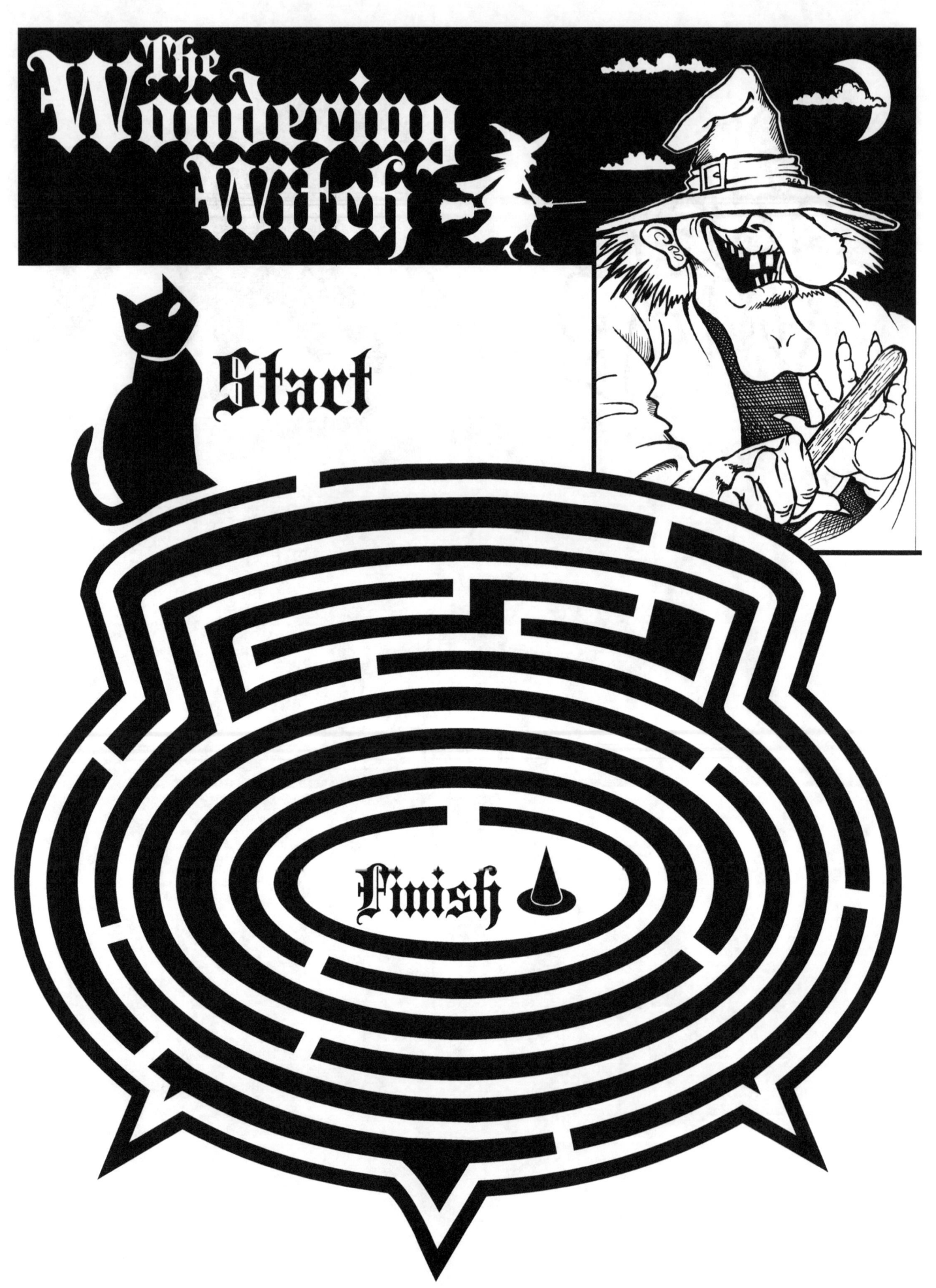

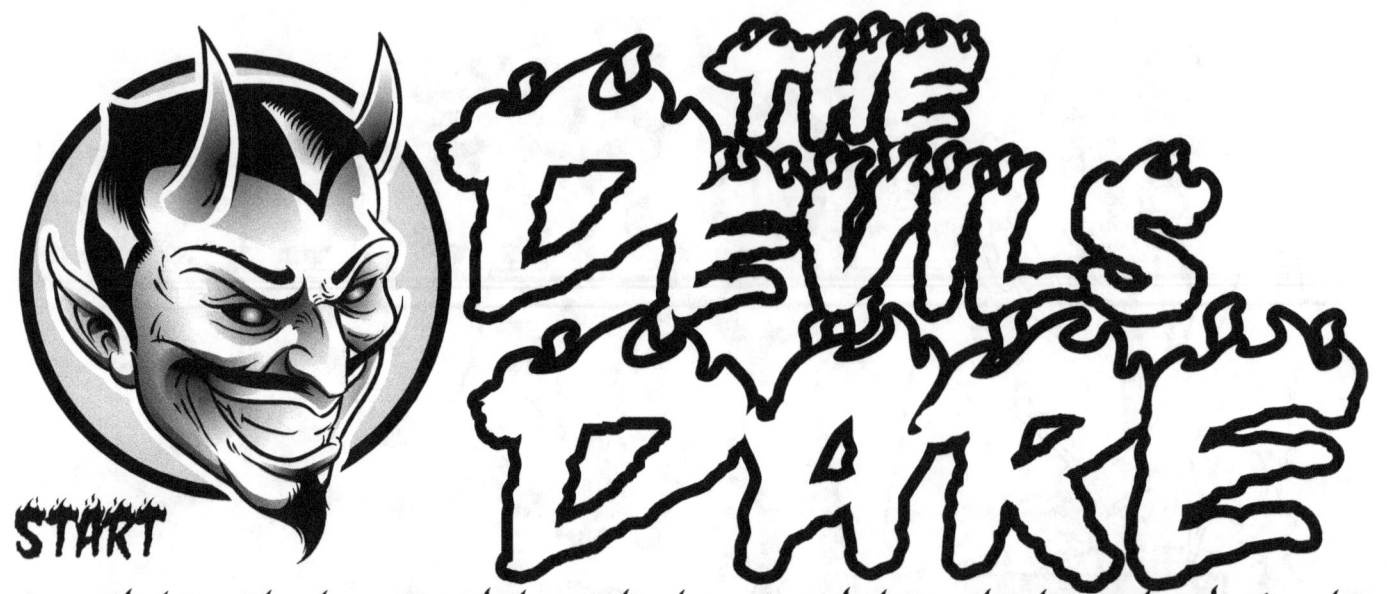

START

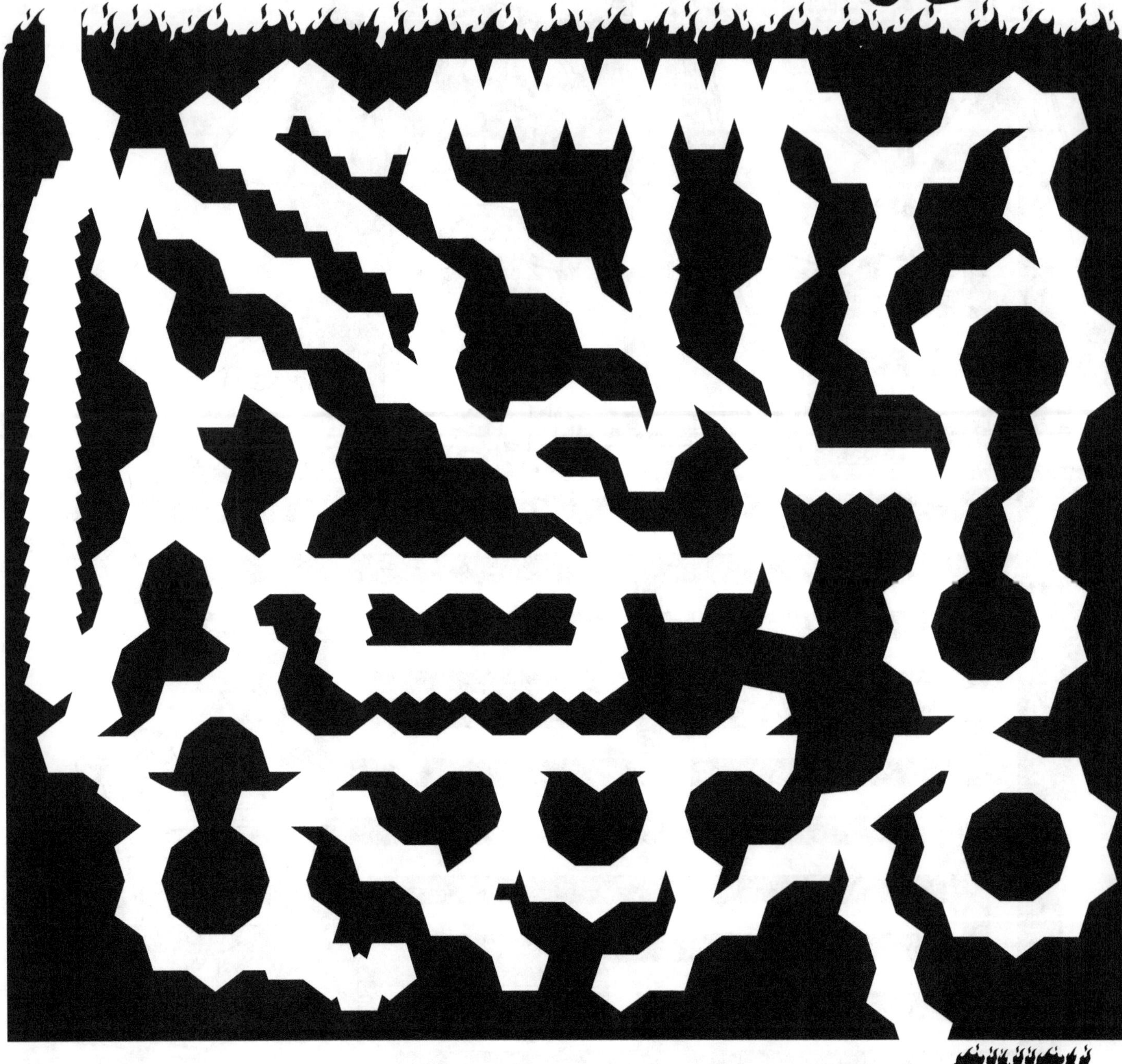

FINISH

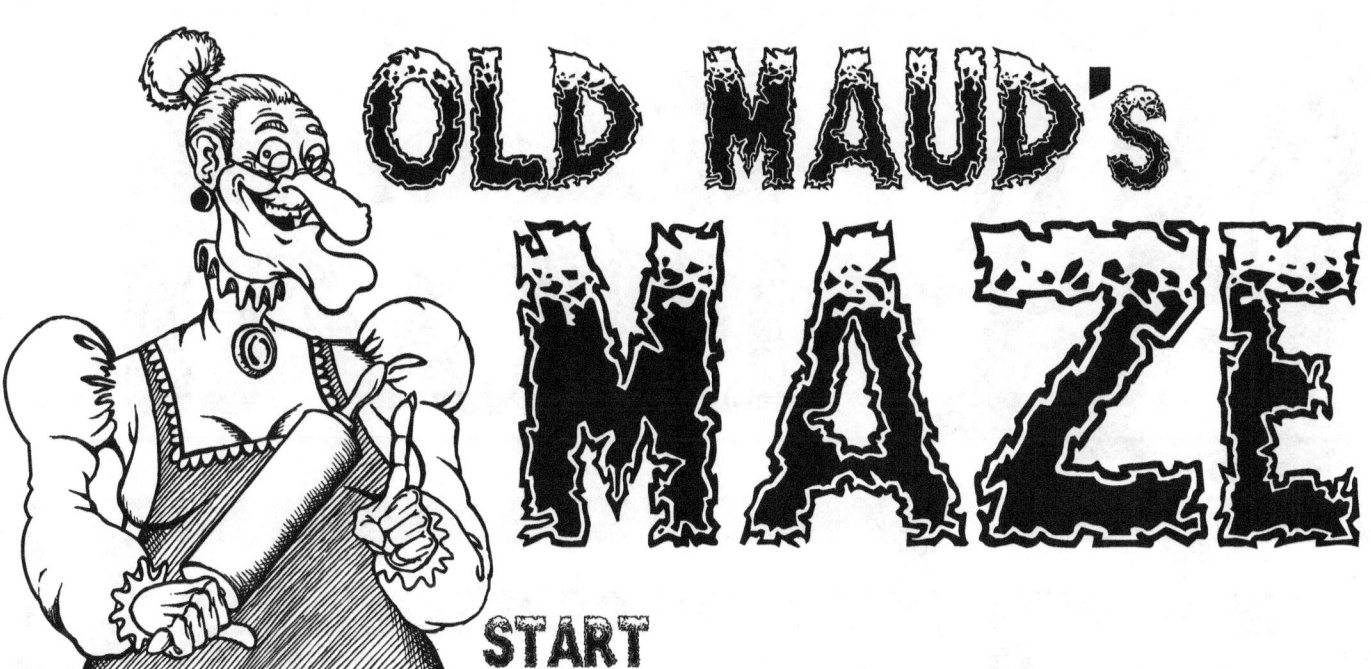

START

FINISH

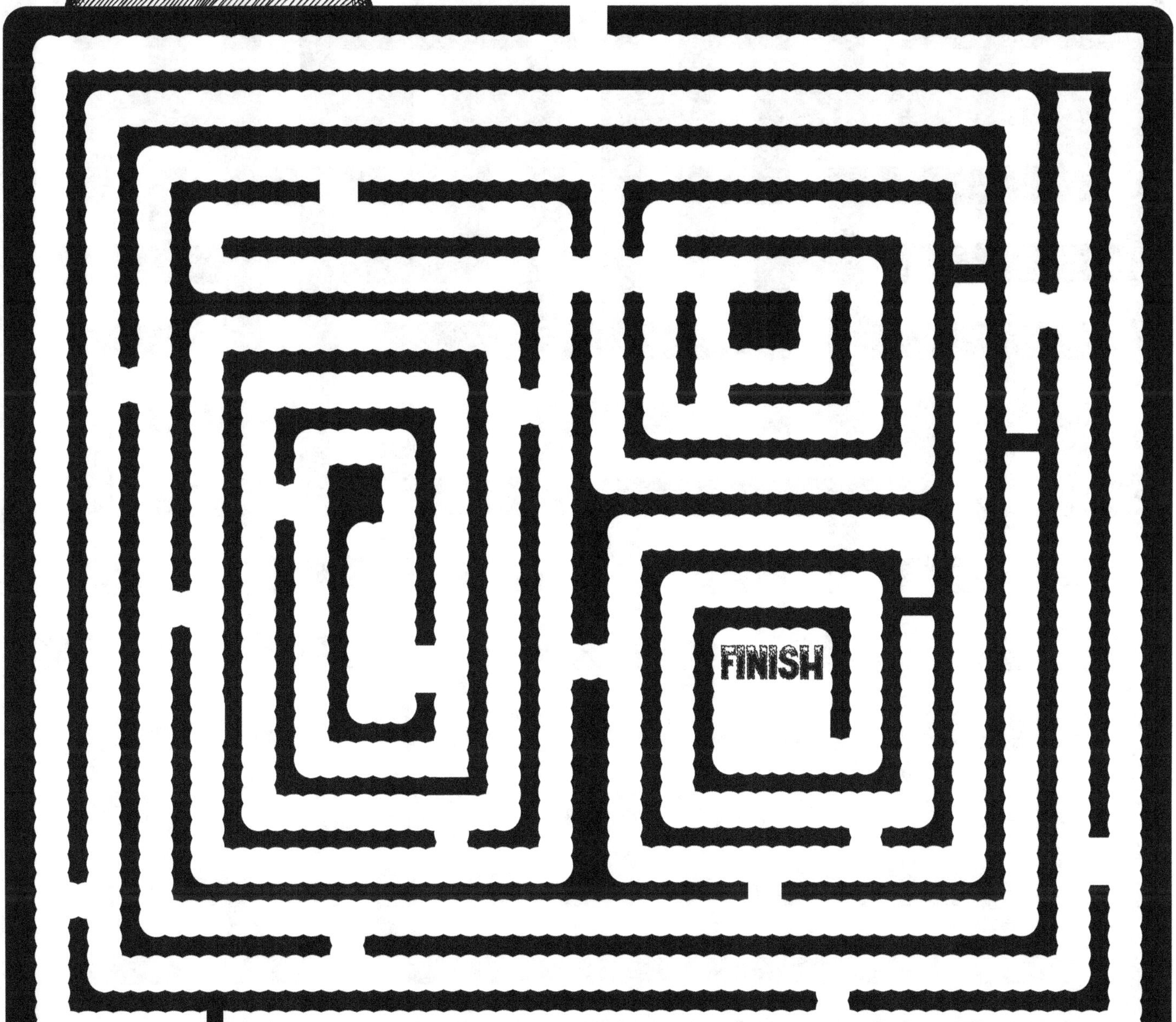

THE MAZE OF THE MOAI

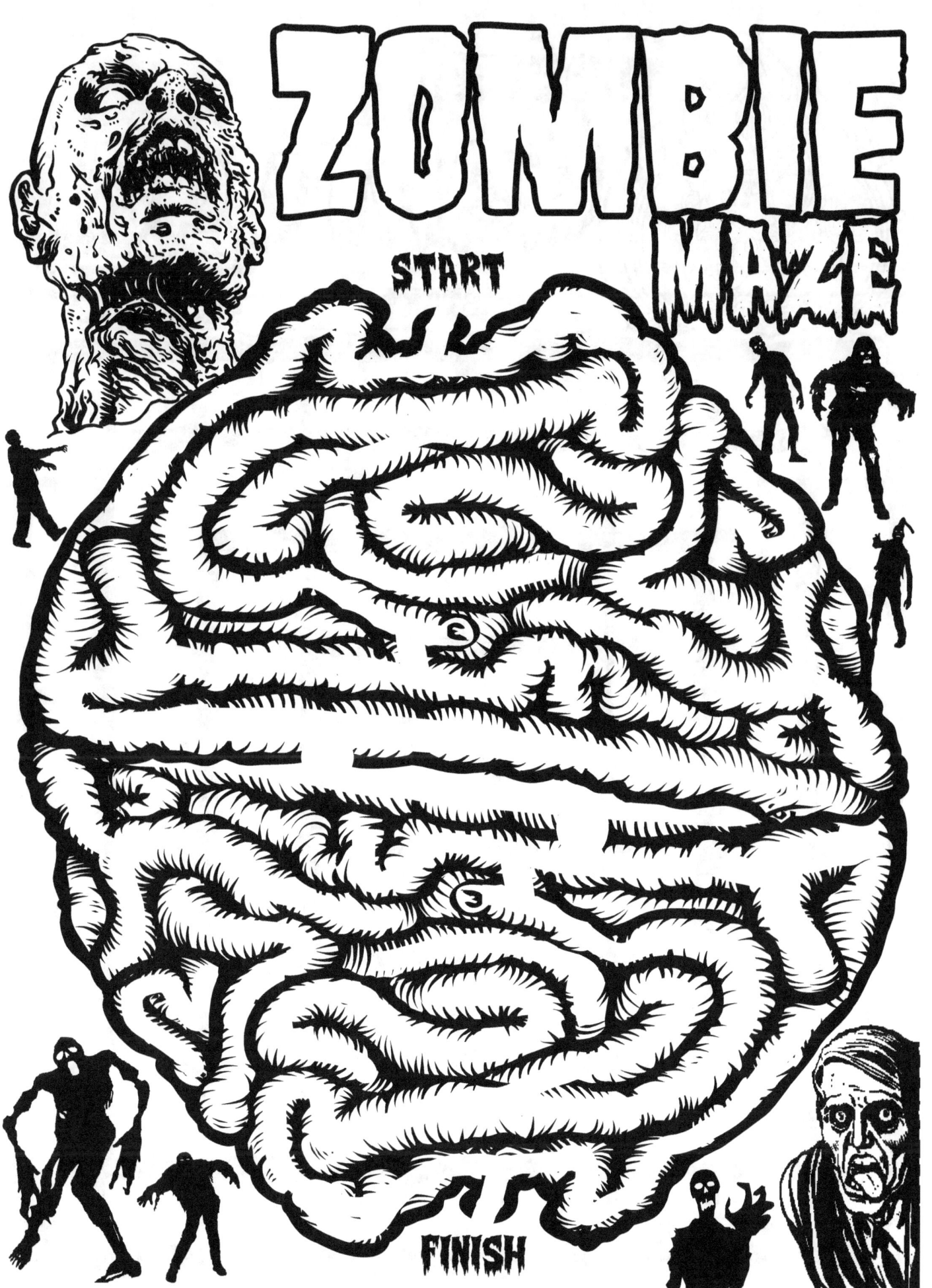

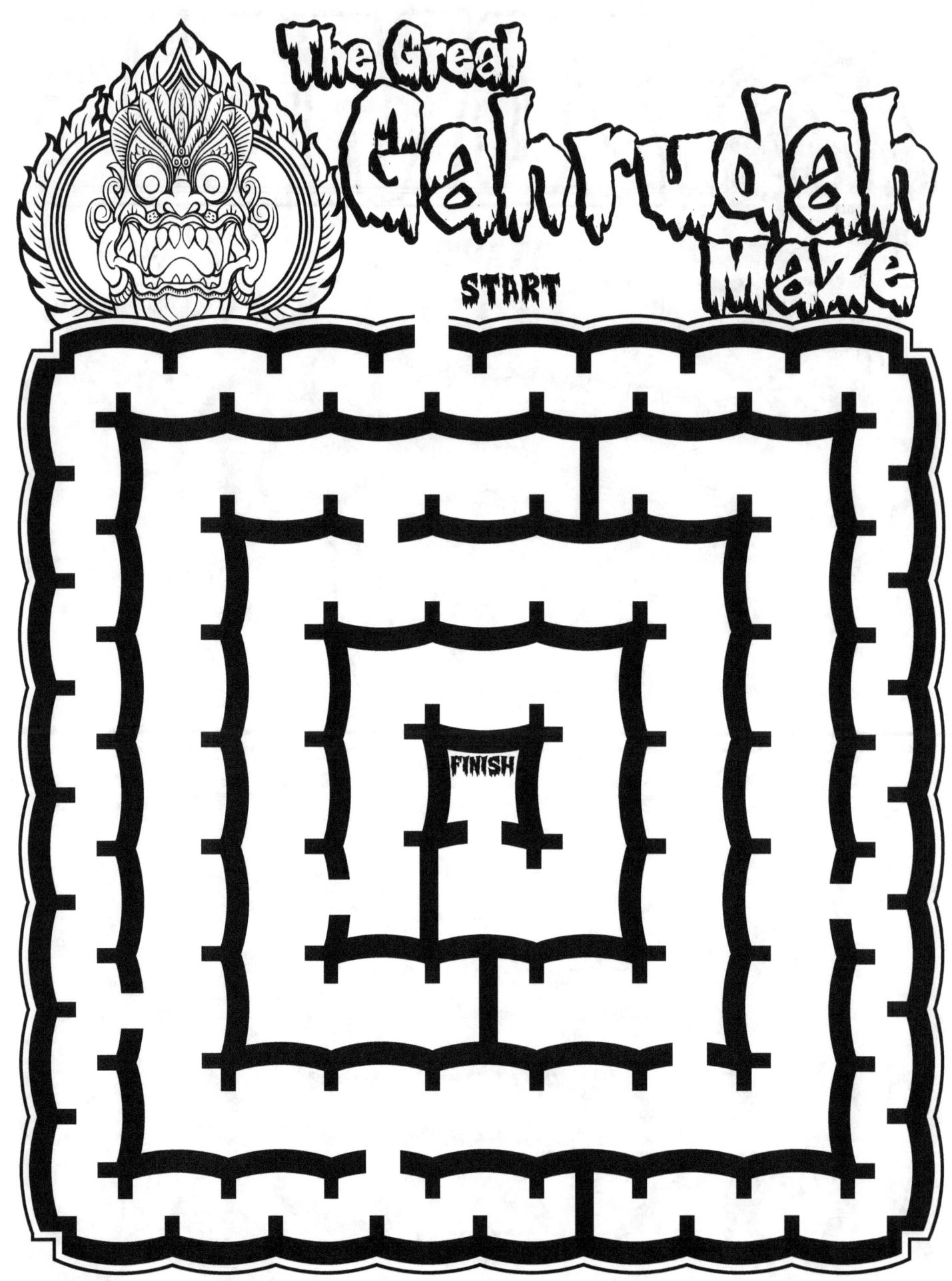

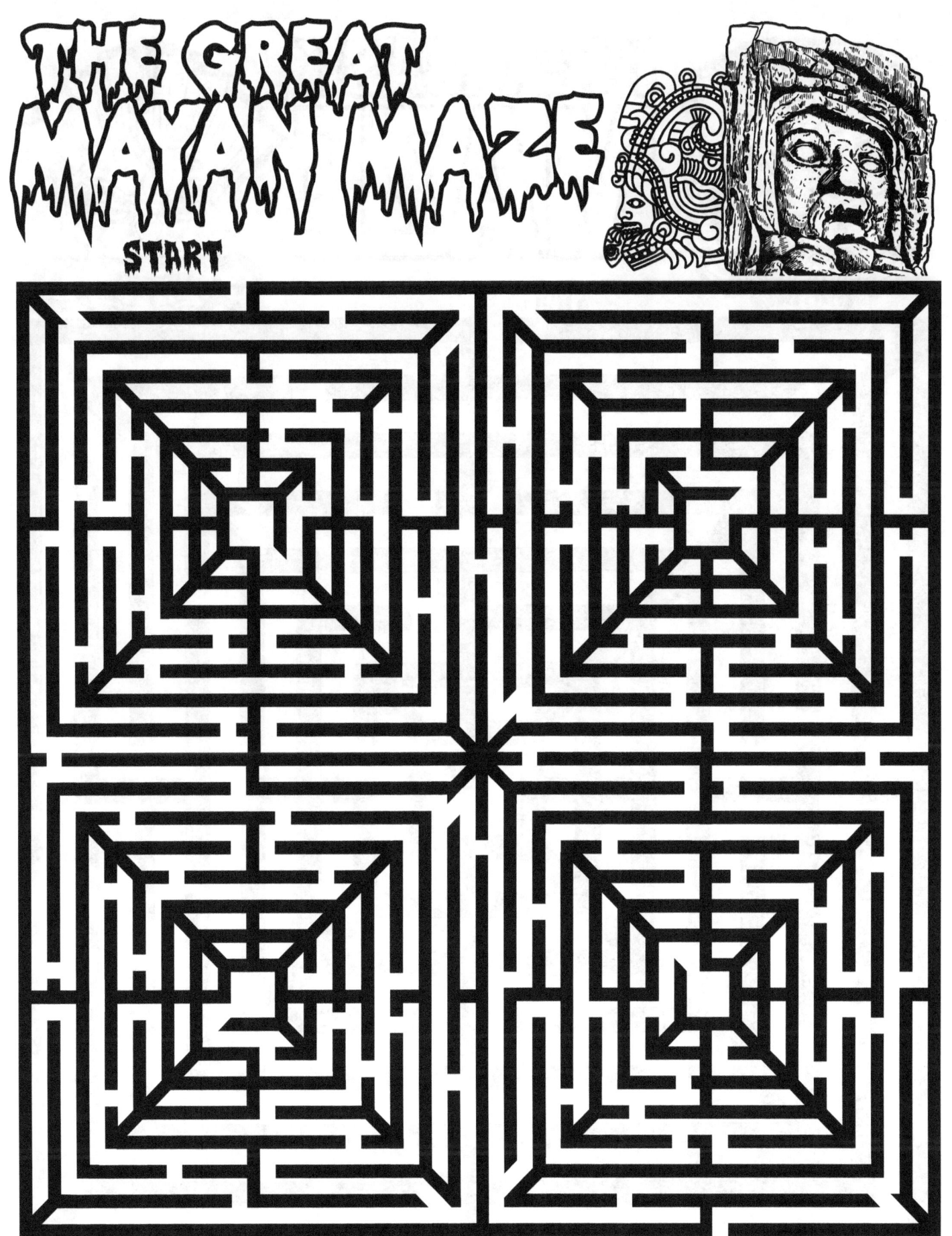

INCA MASK
MAZE

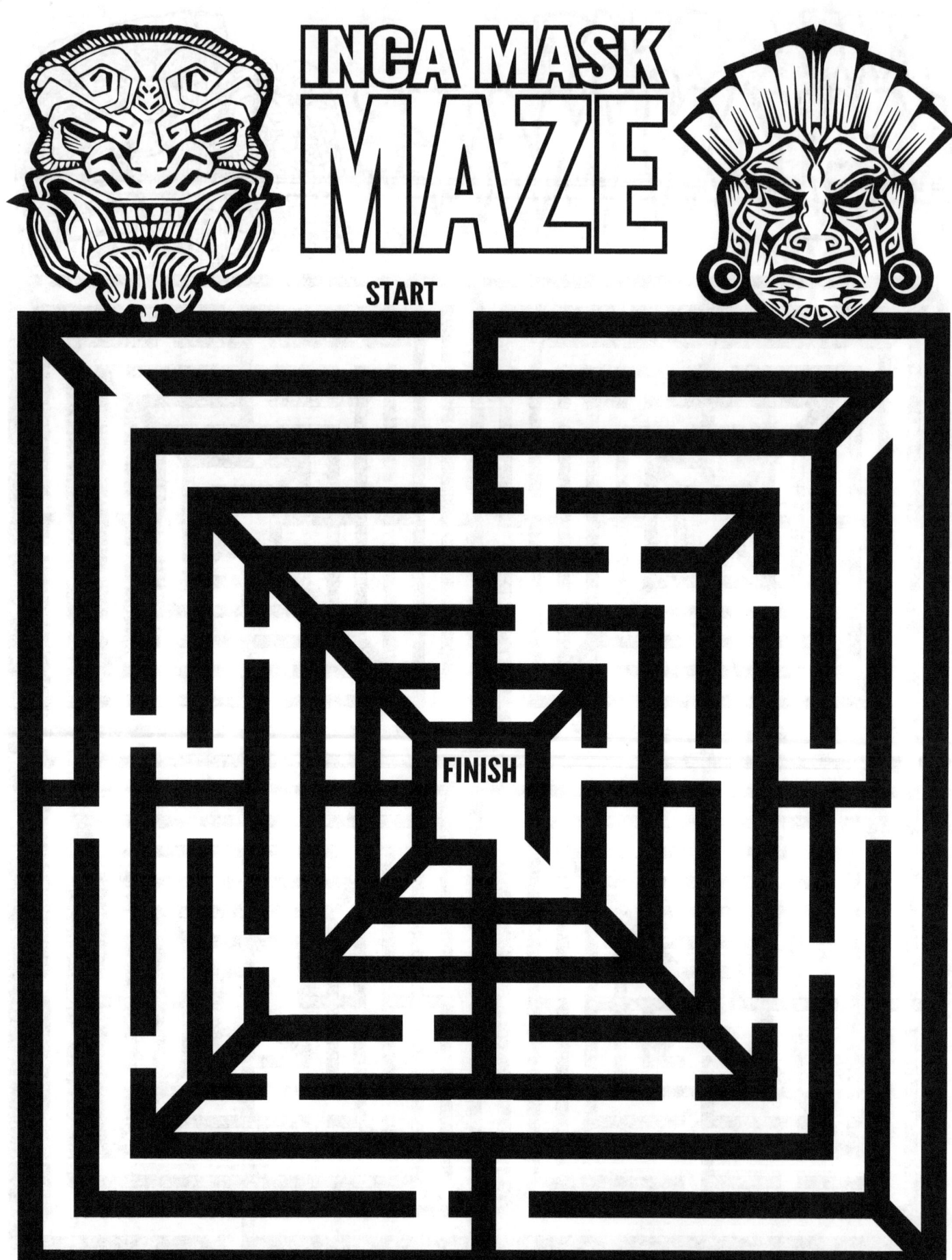

START

FINISH

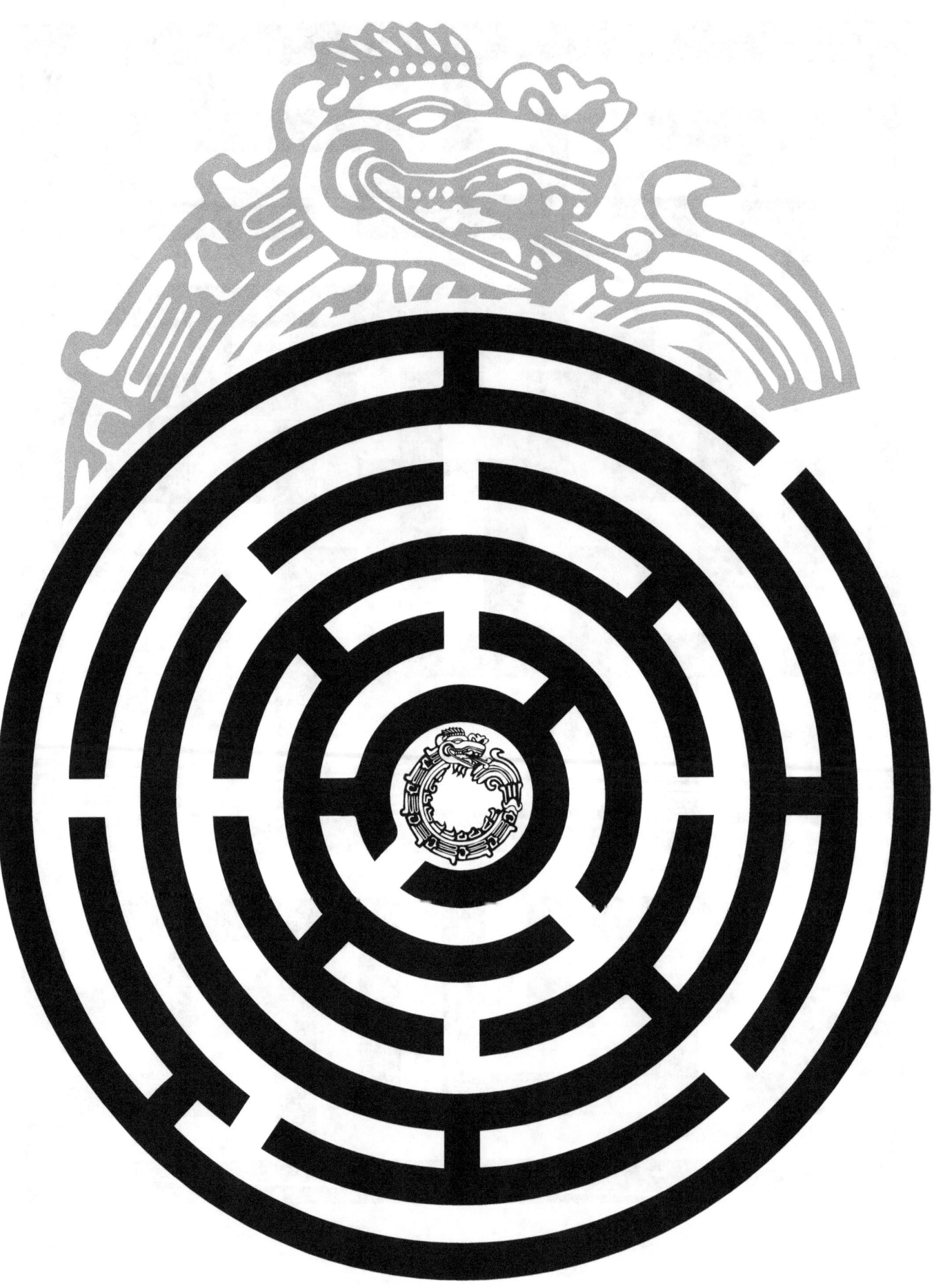

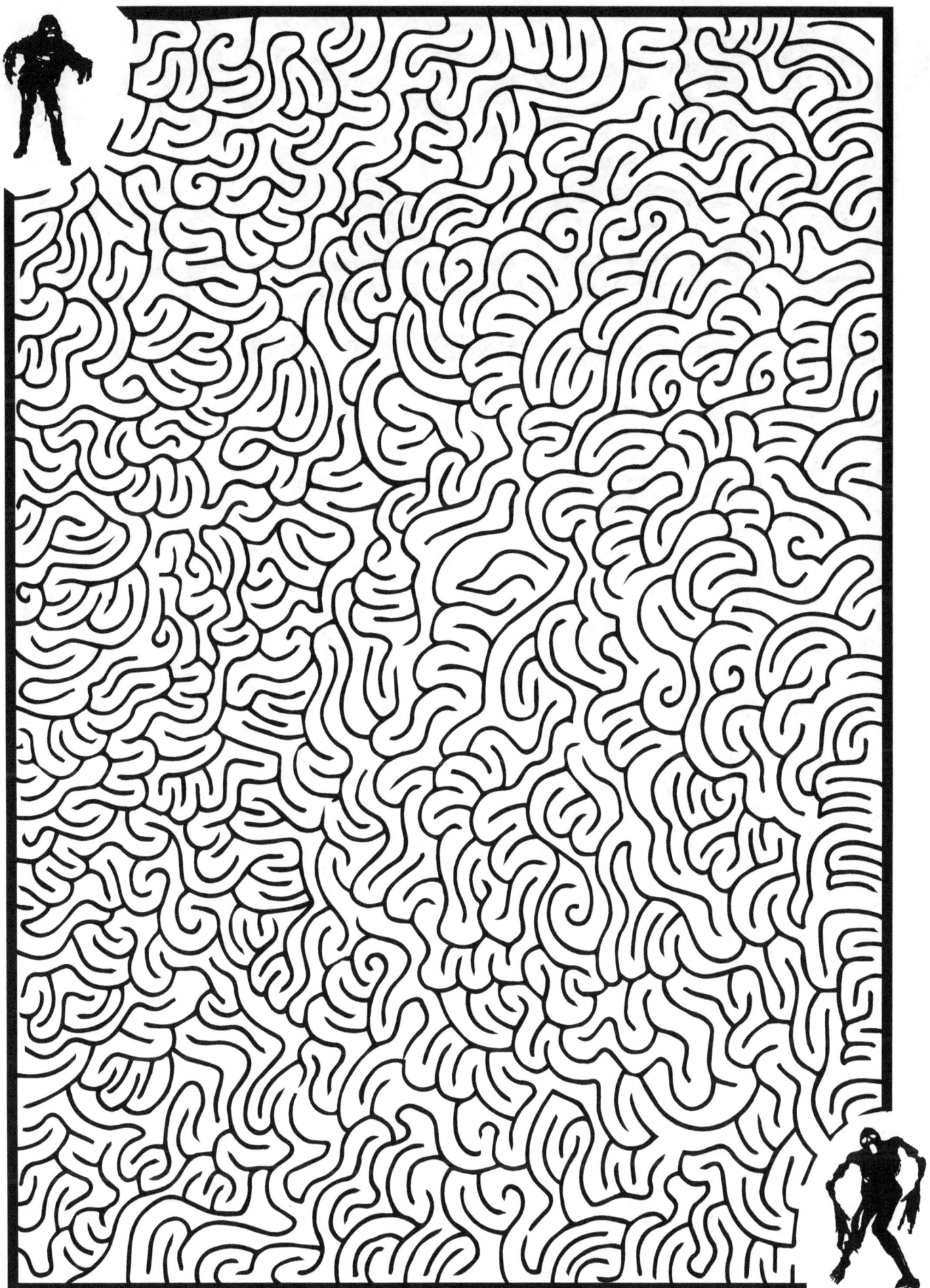

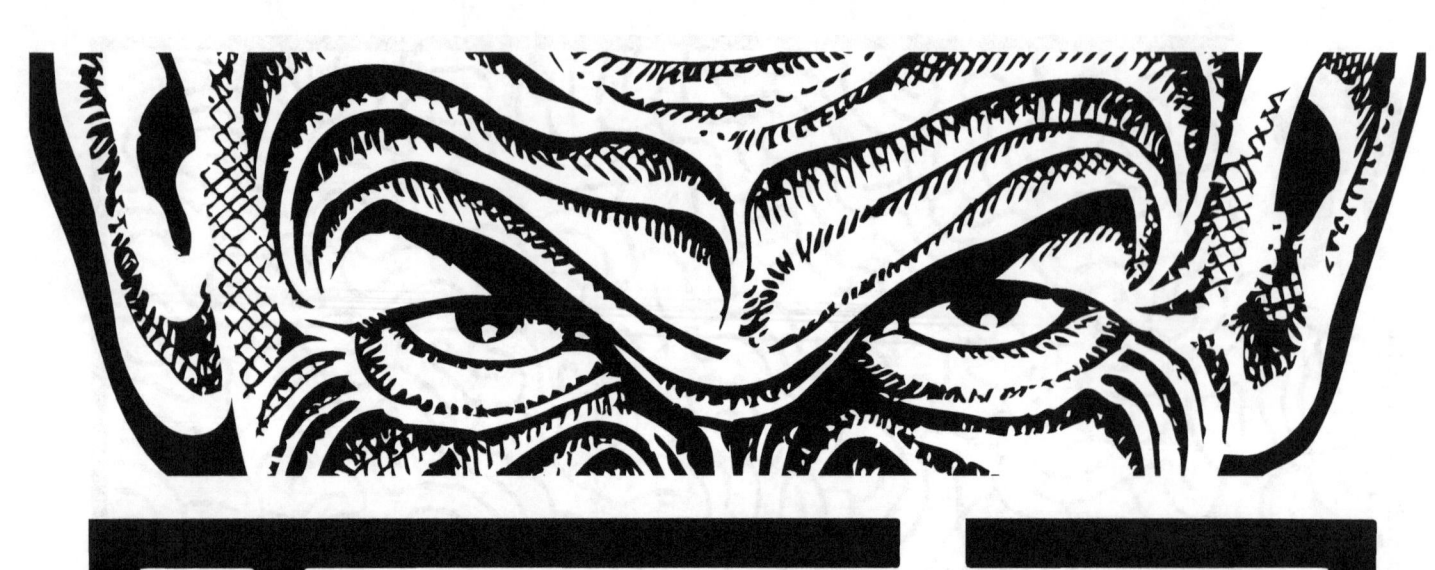

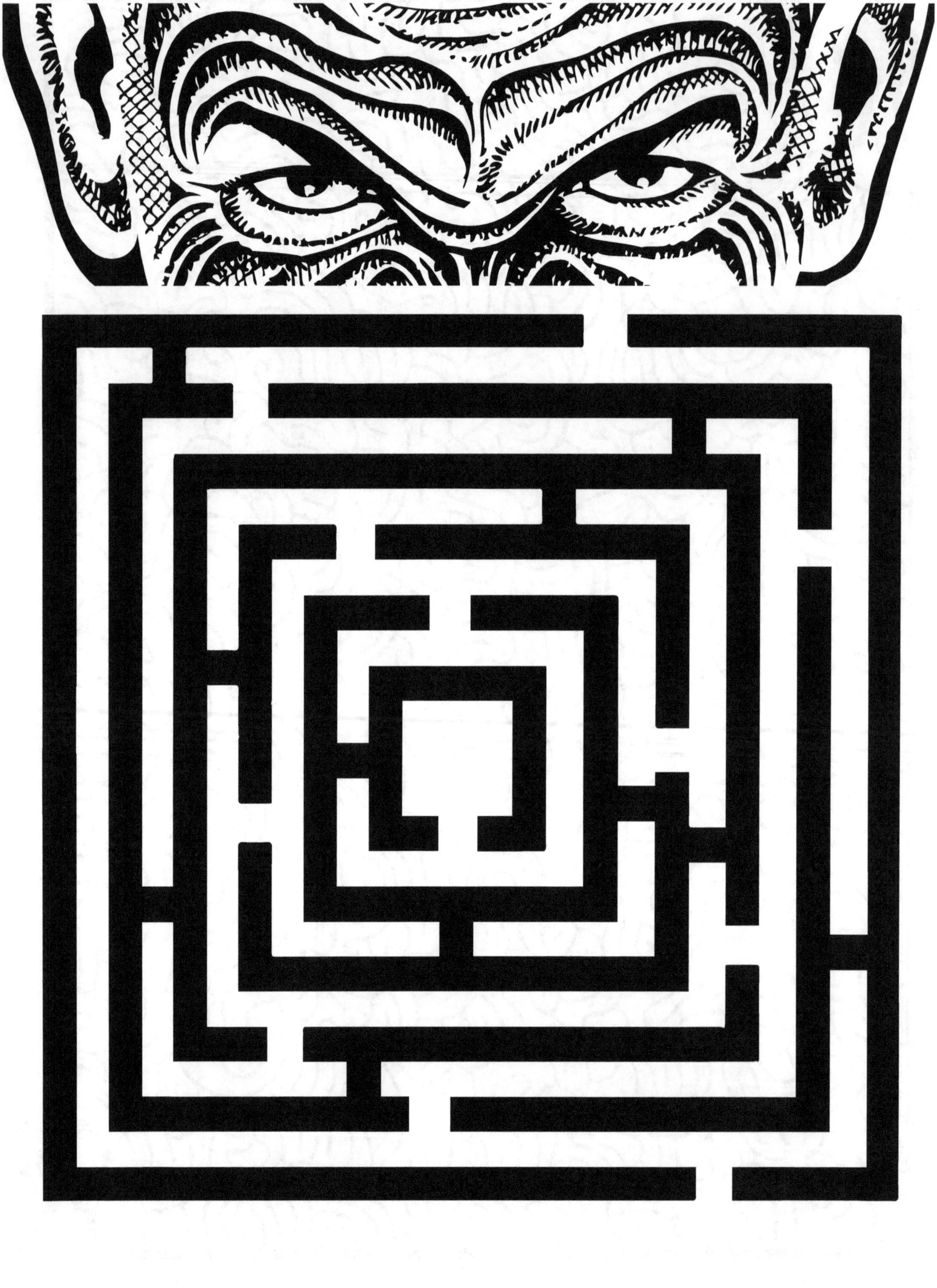

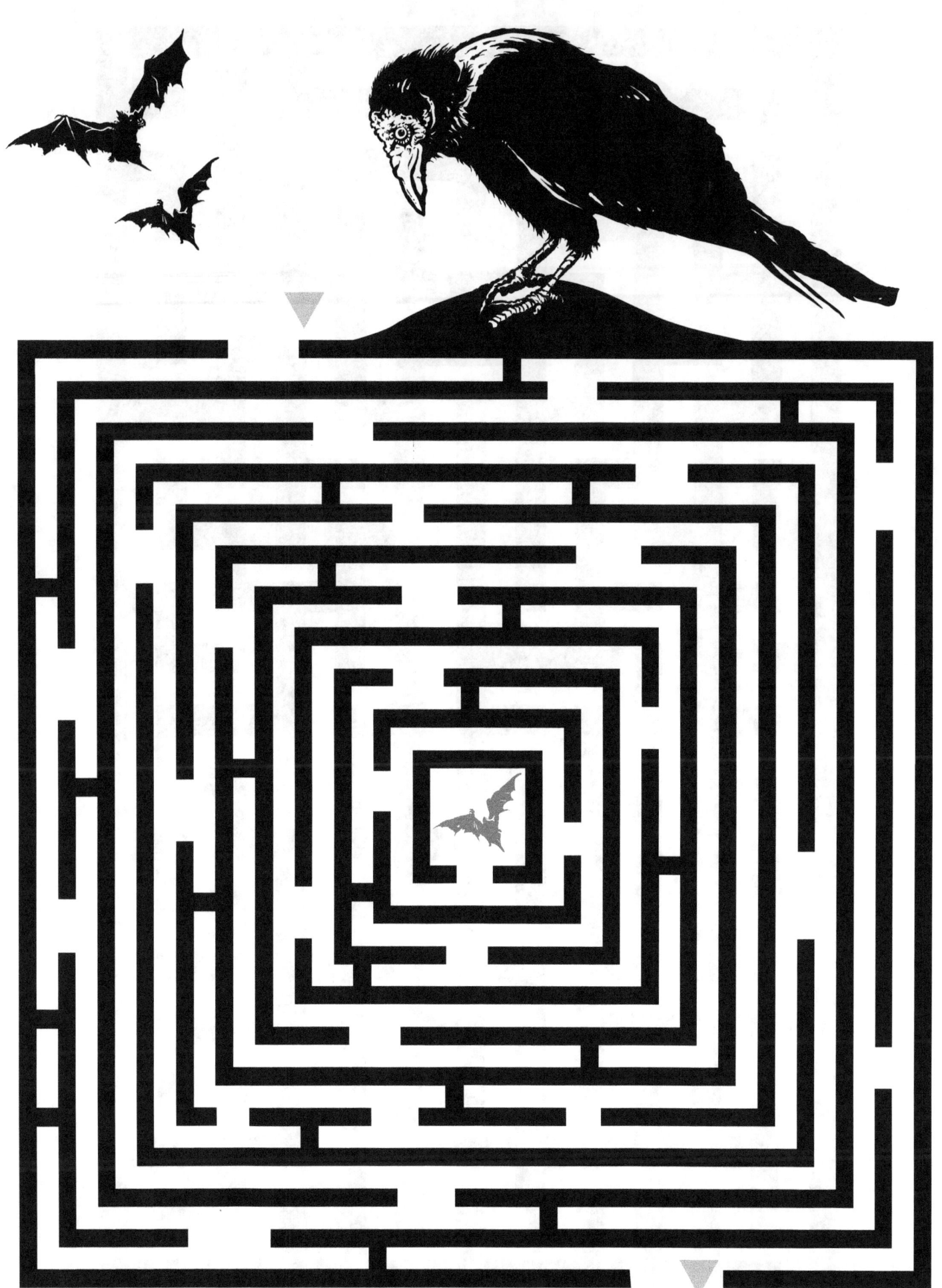

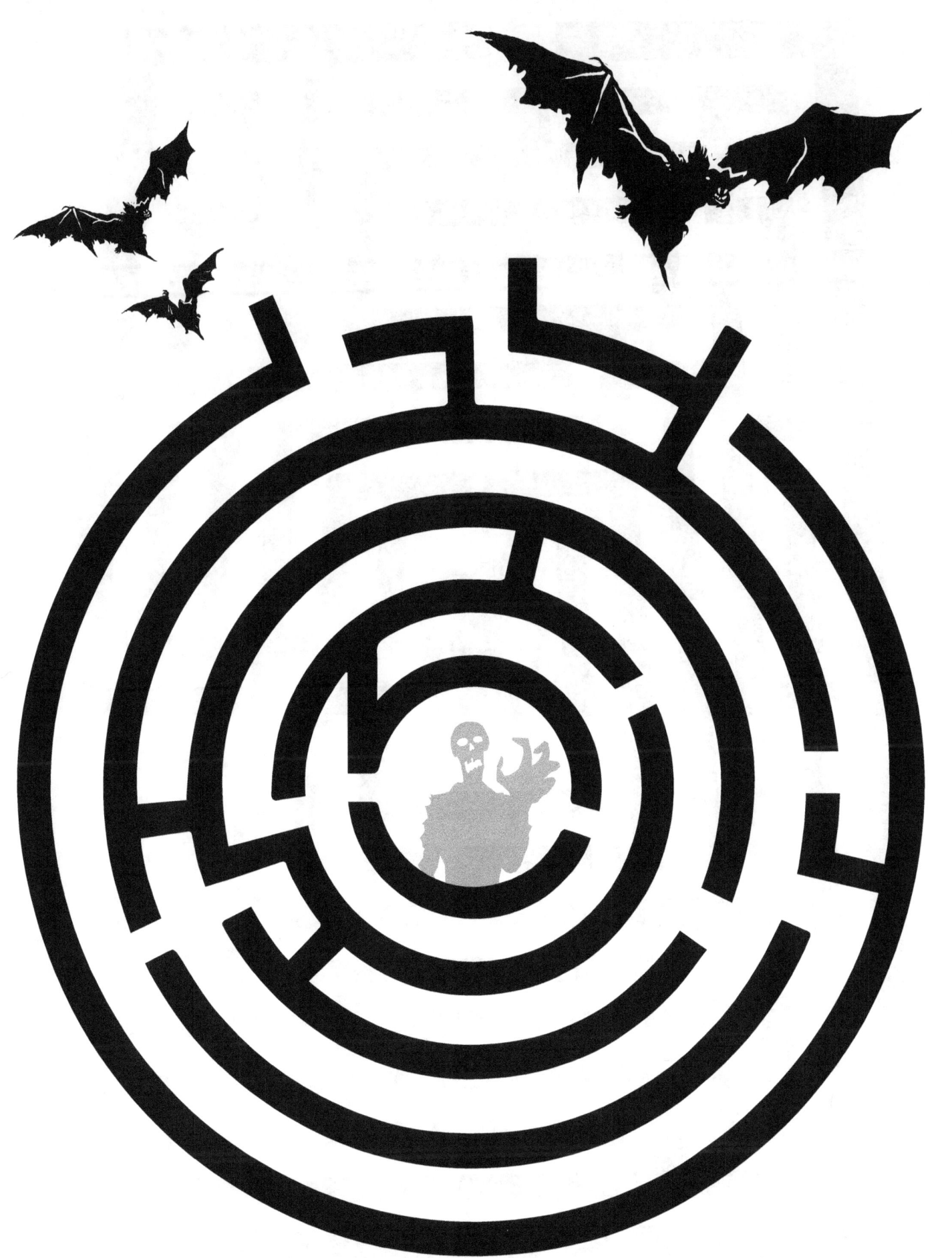

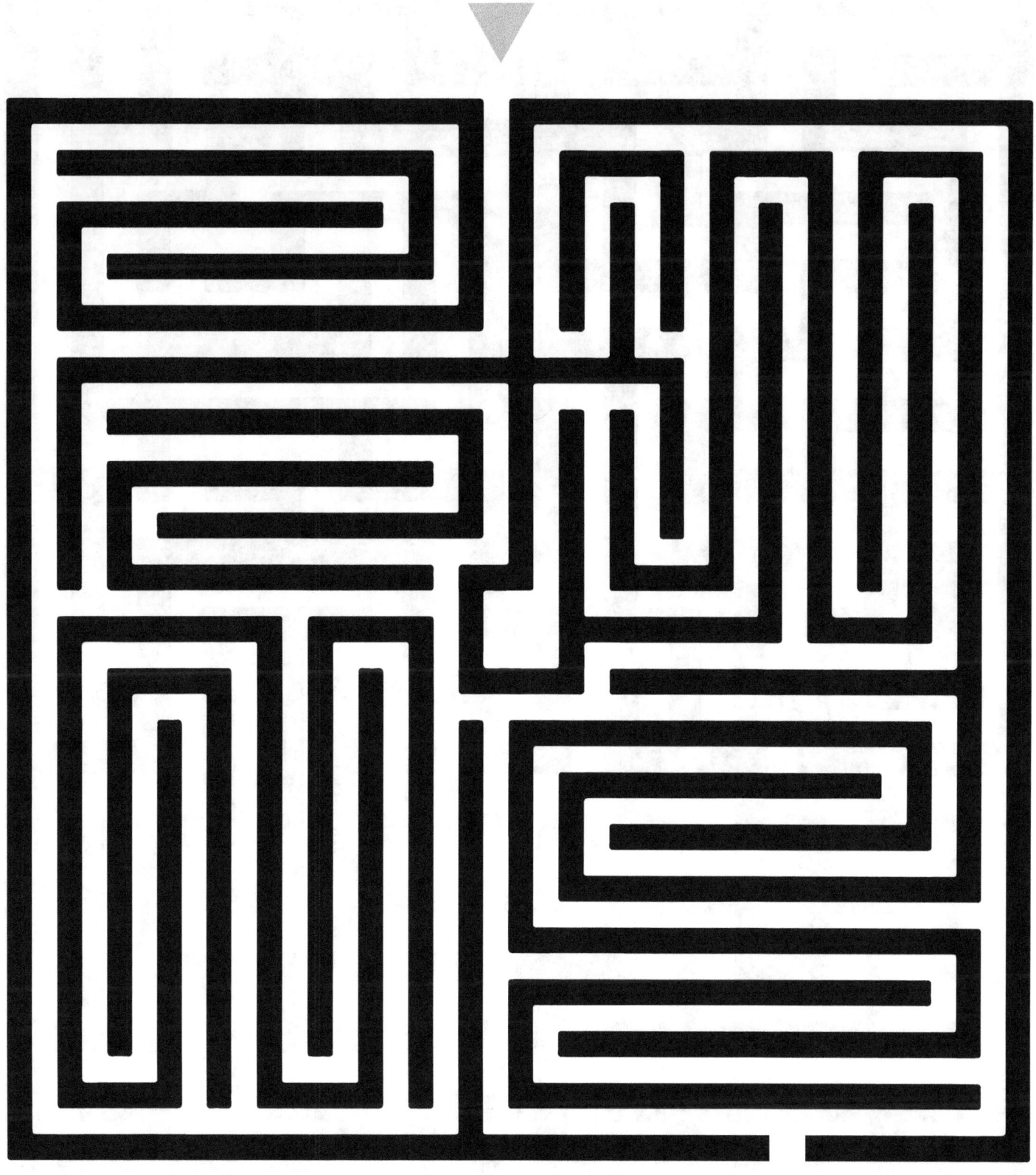

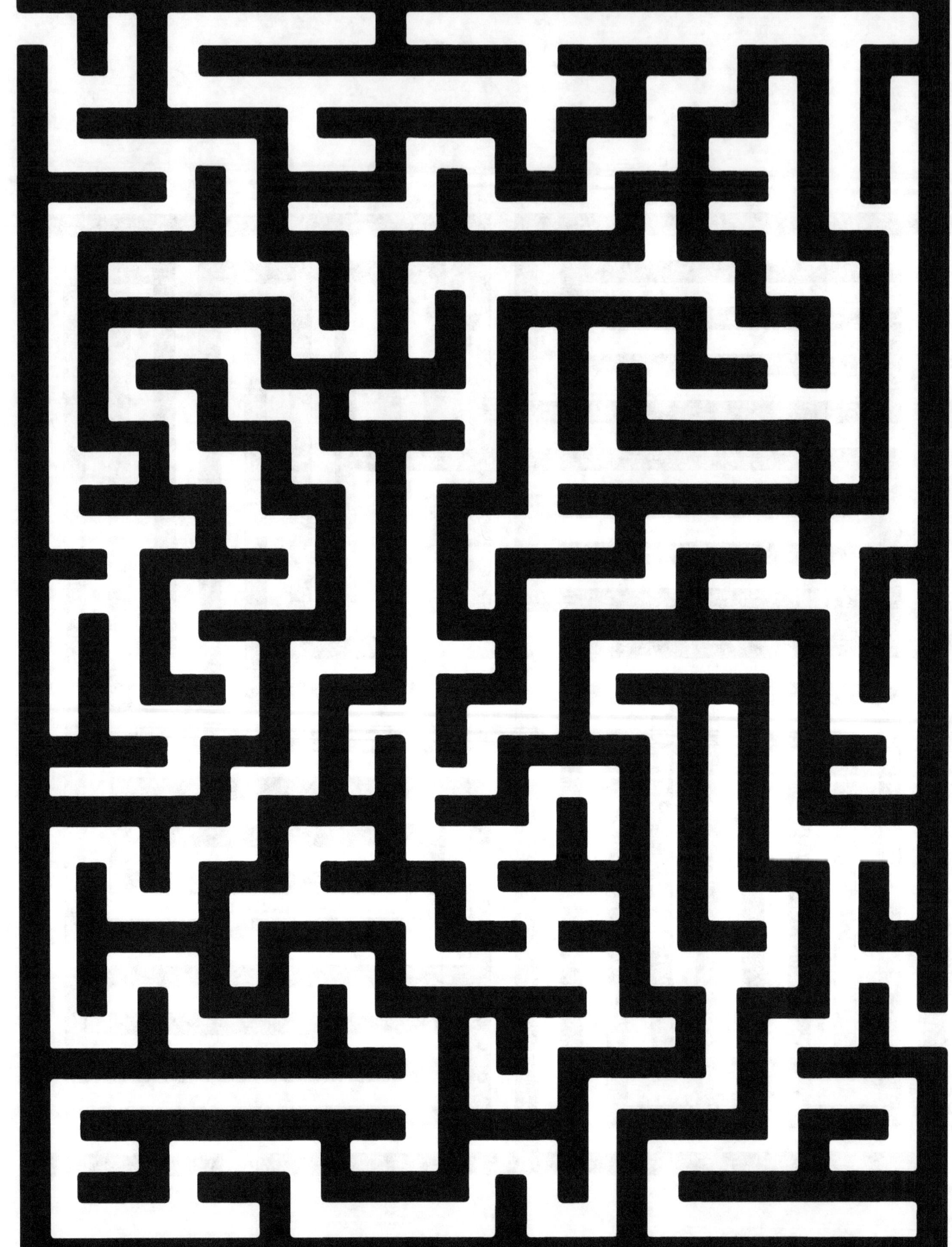

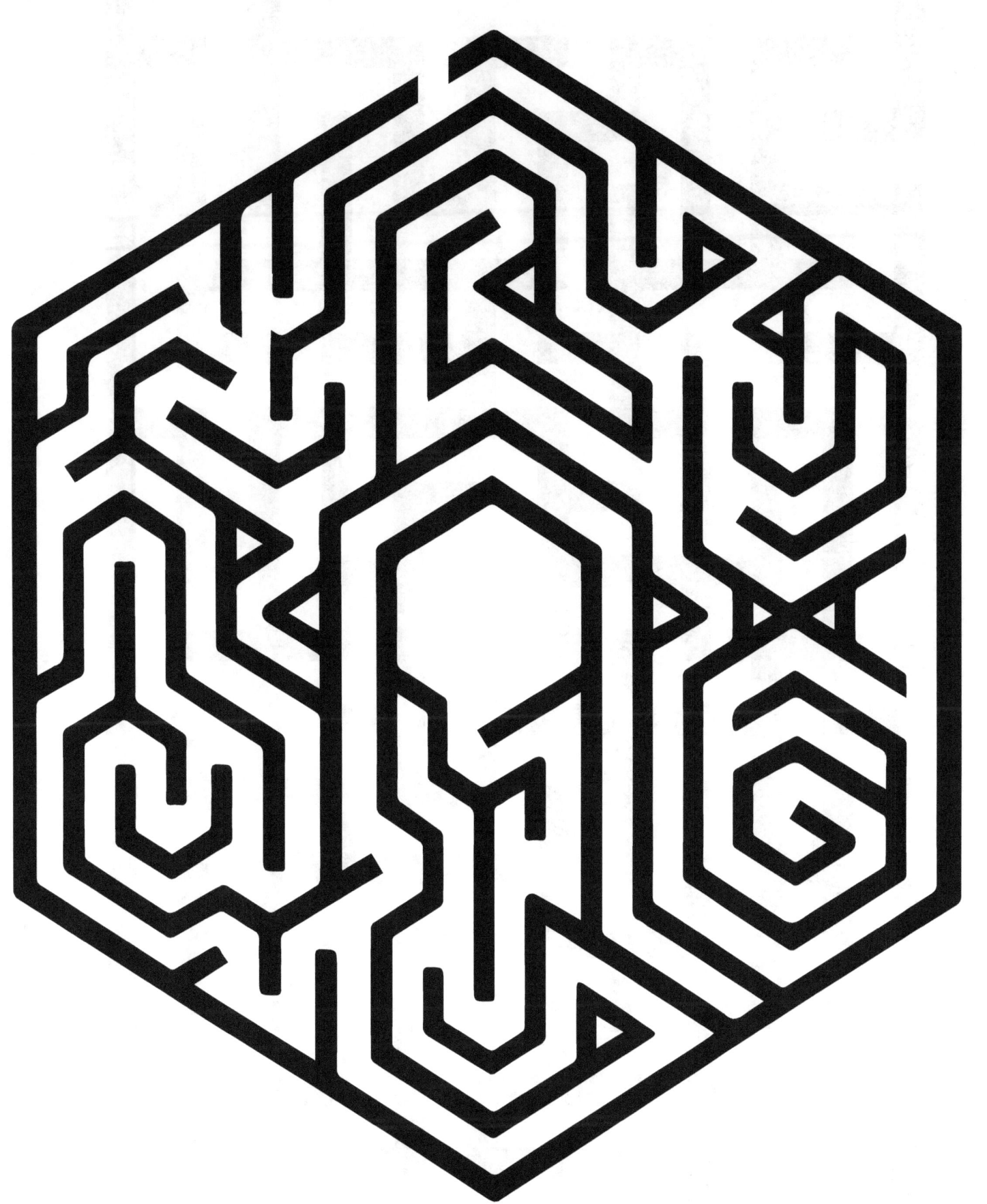

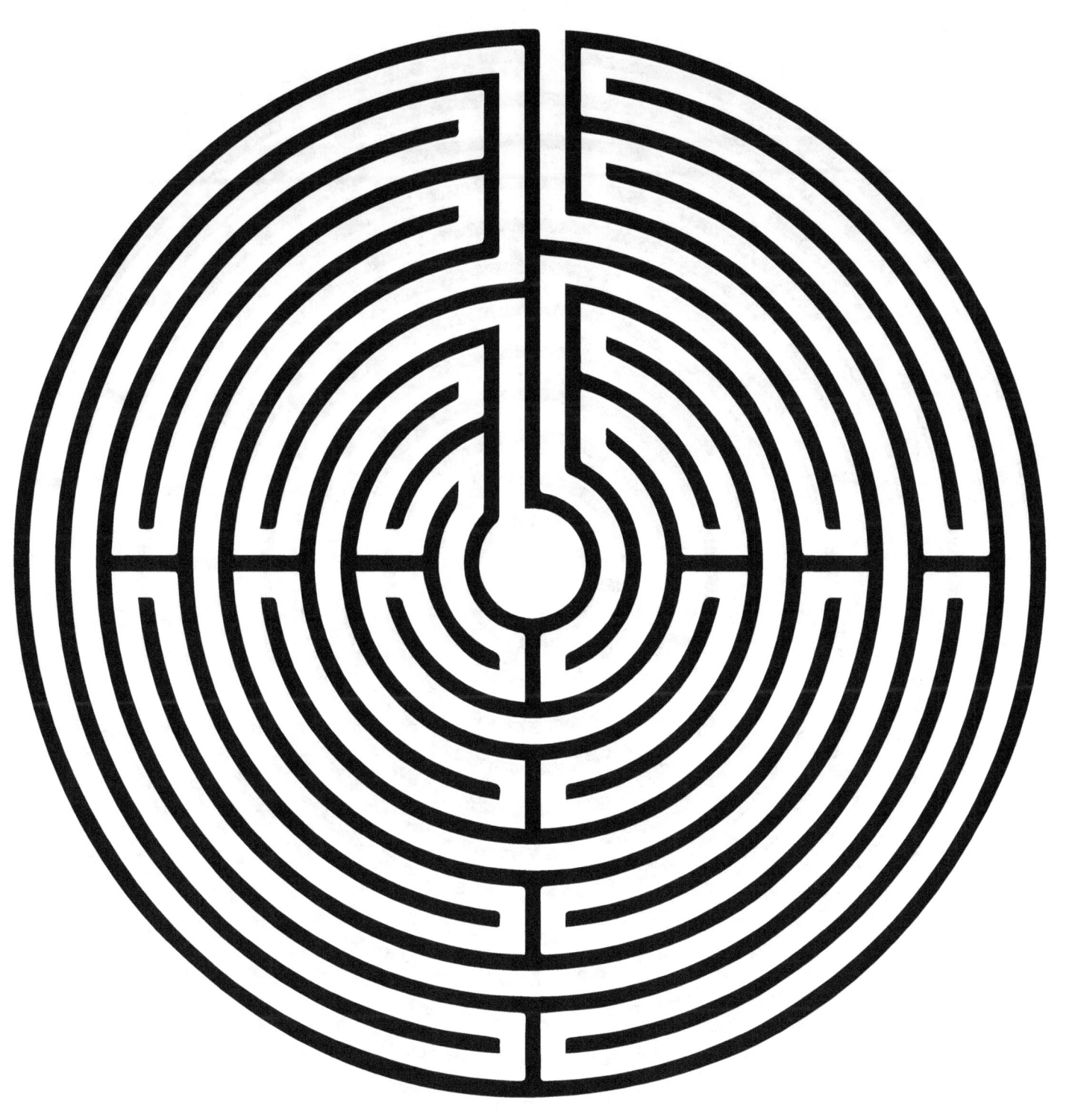

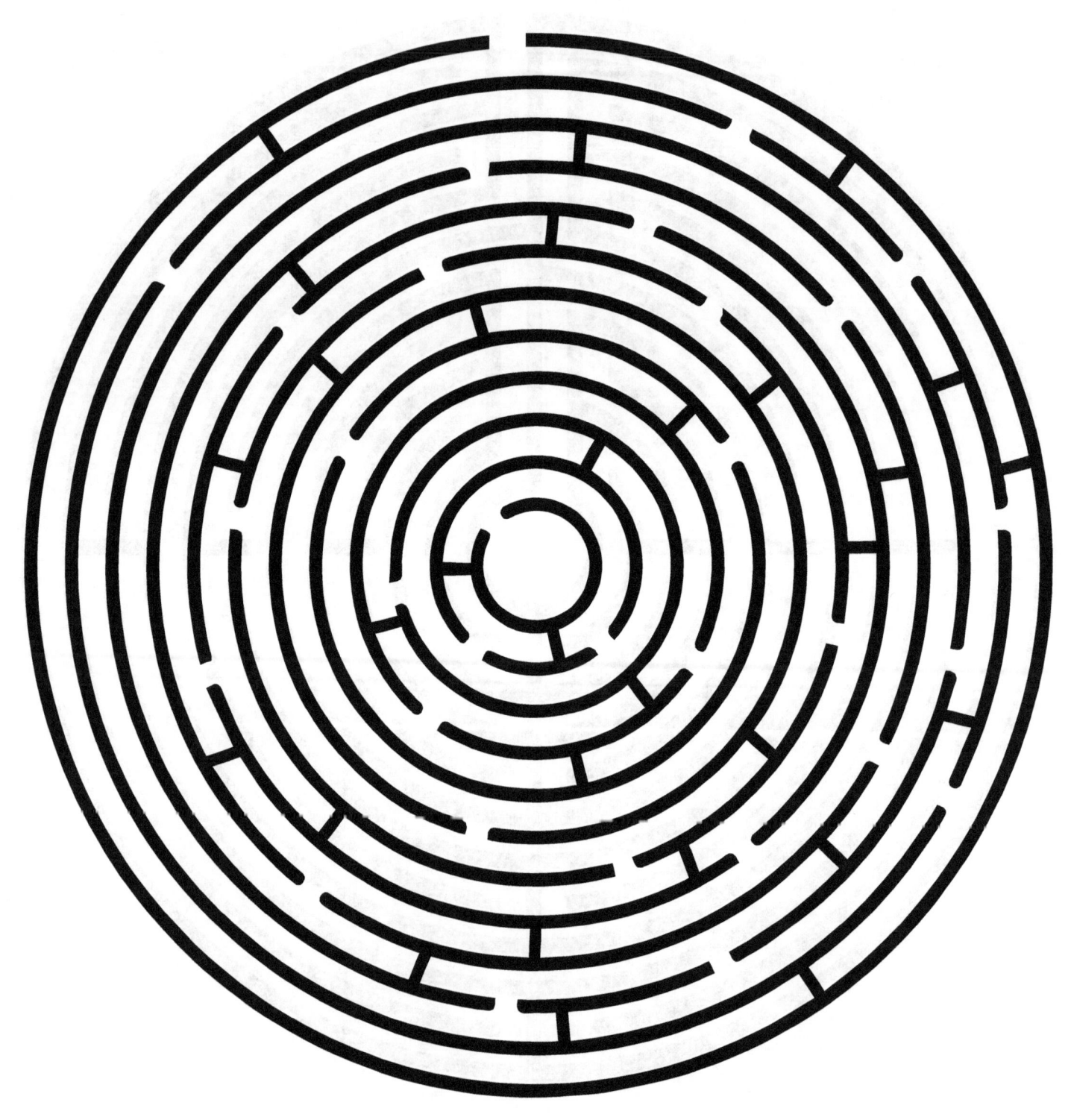

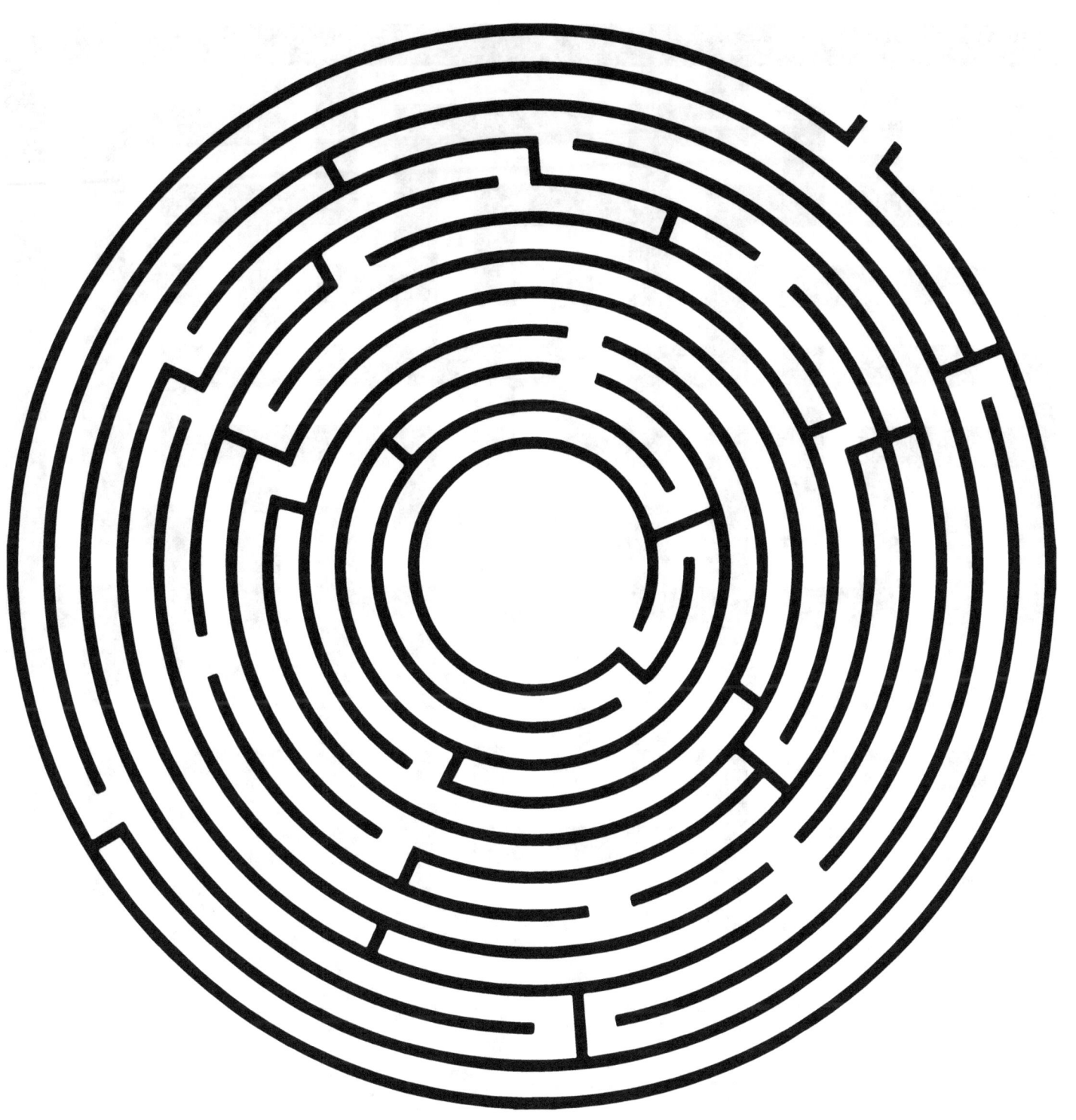

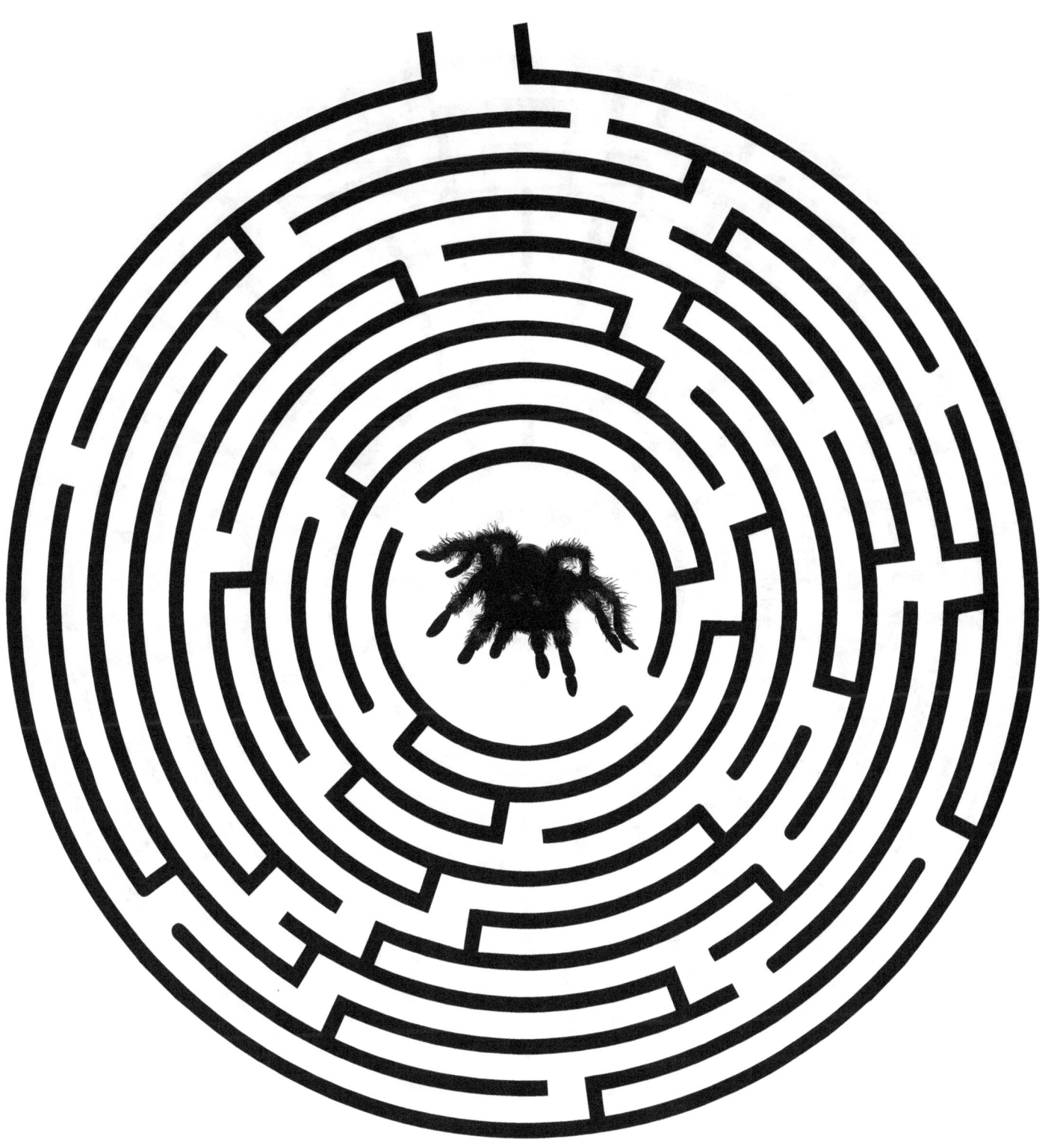

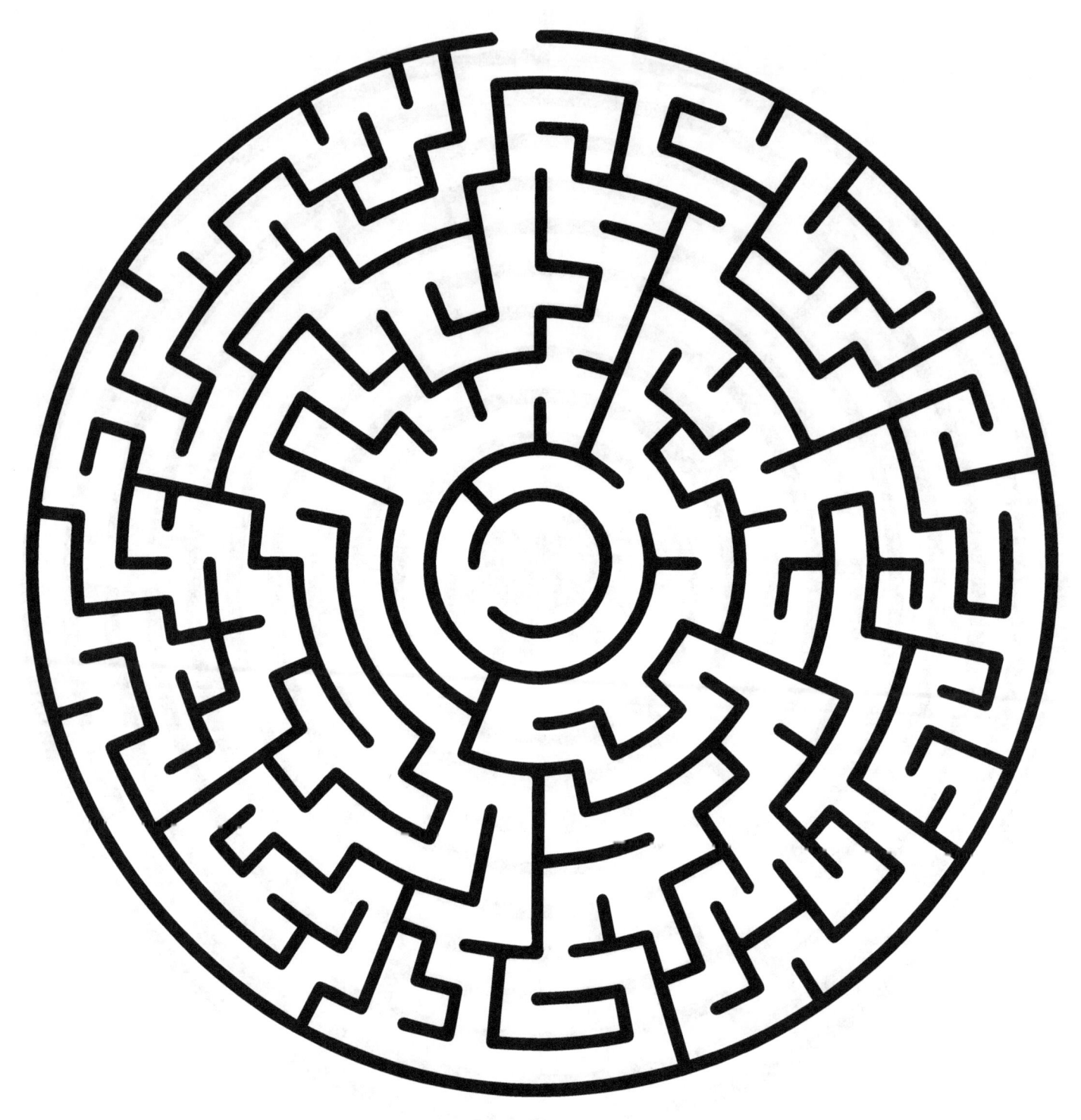

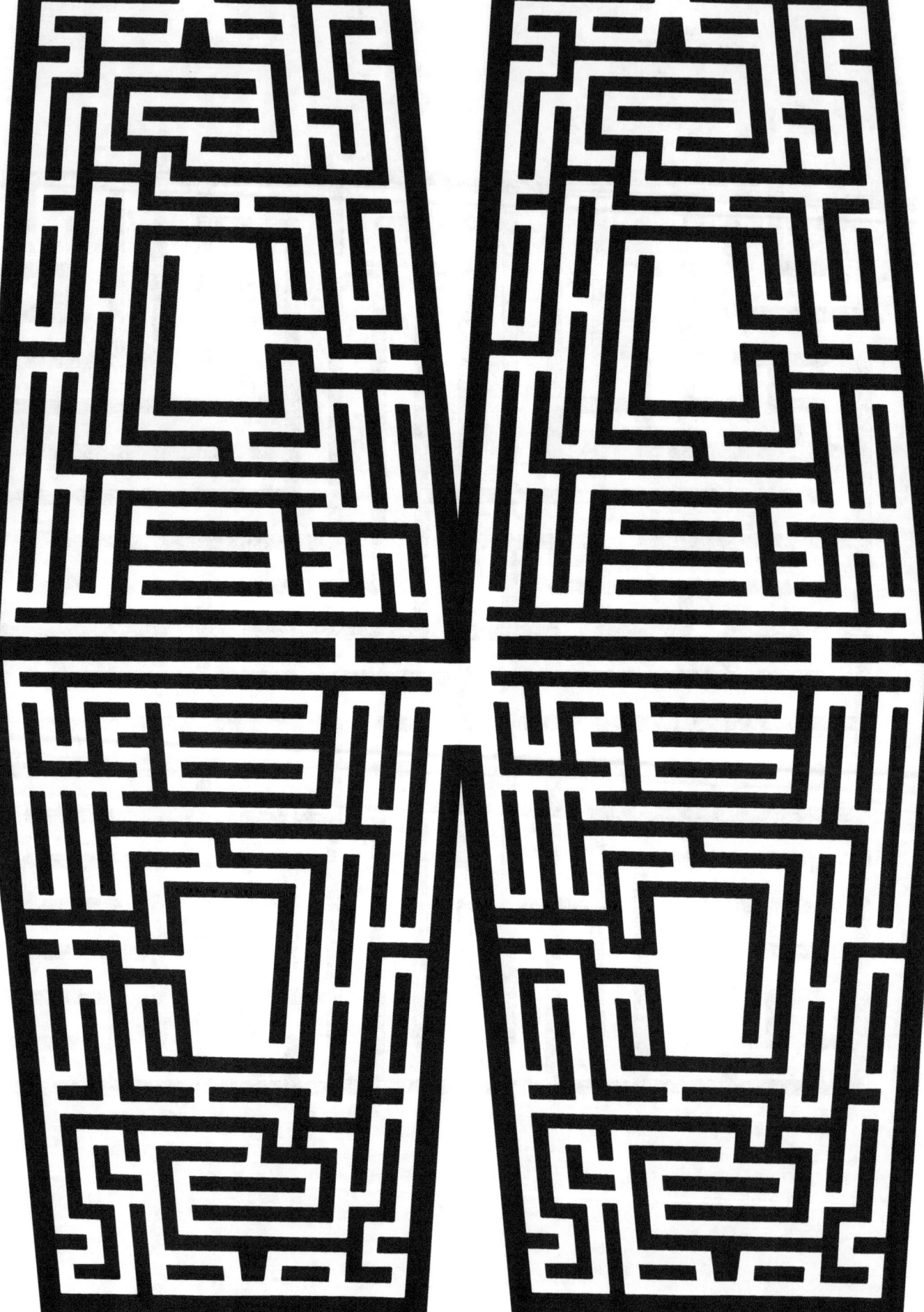

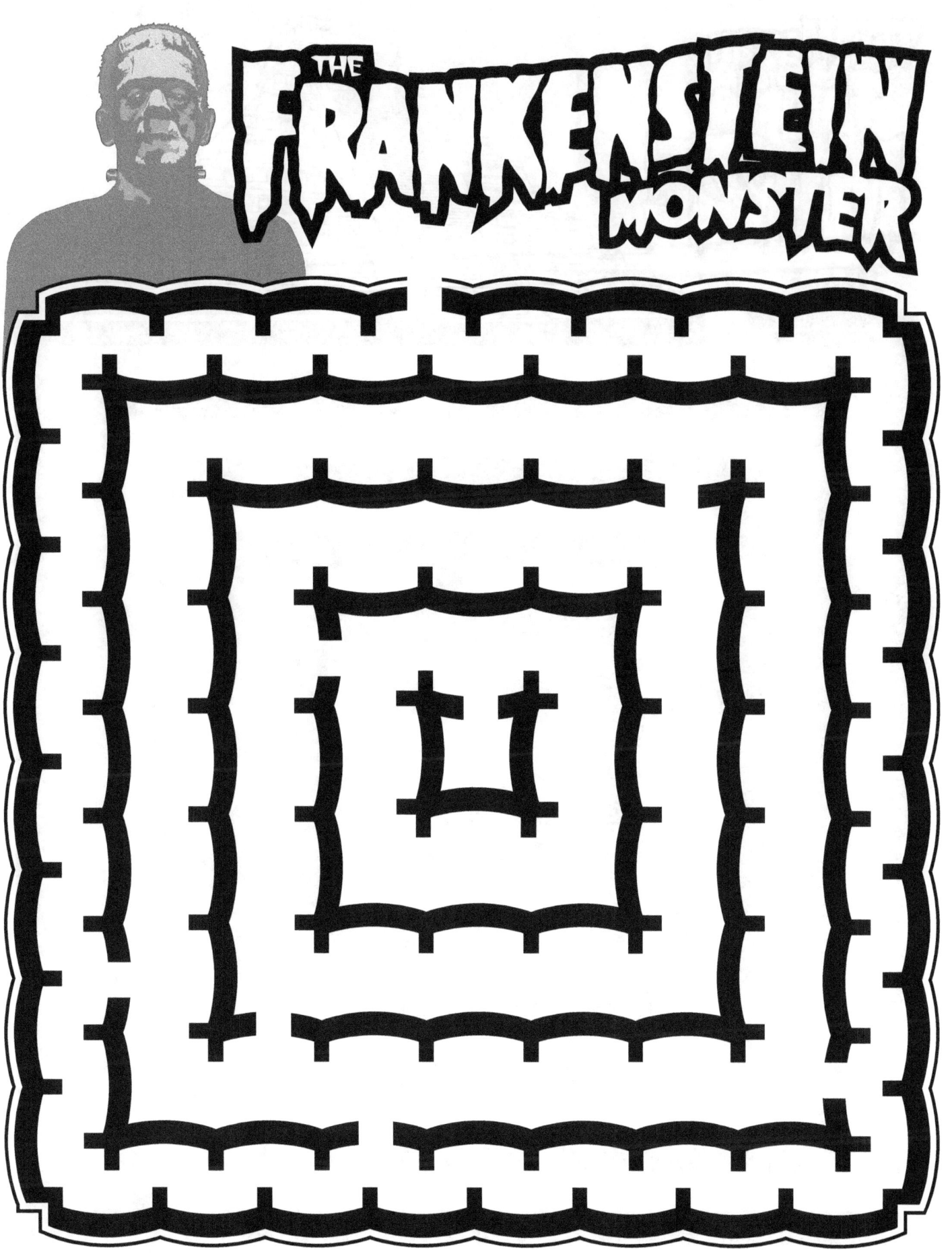

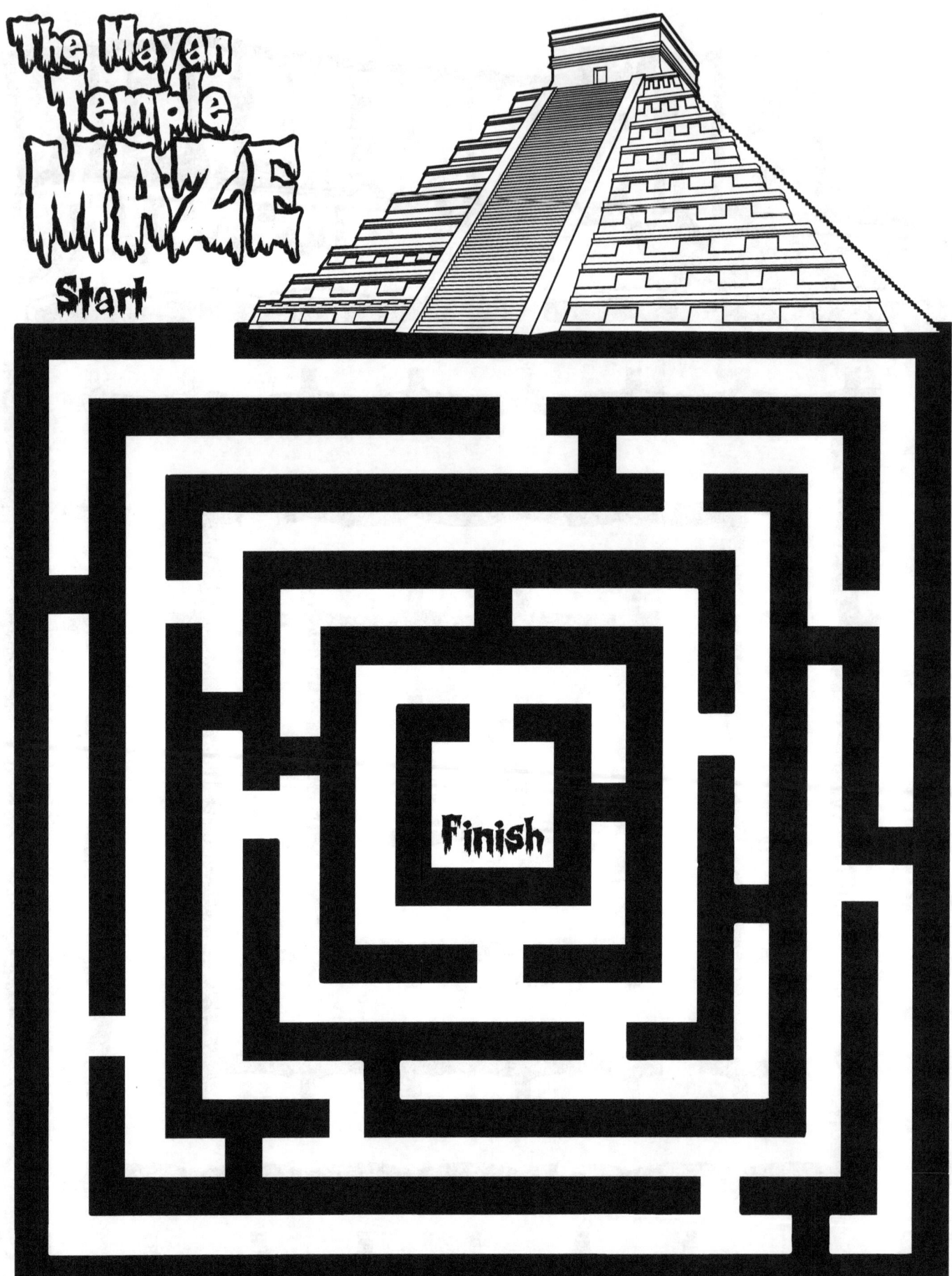

START

THE
COFFIN
MAZE

FINISH

www.ingramcontent.com/pod-product-compliance
Lightning Source LLC
Chambersburg PA
CBHW080617180526
45168CB00007B/2950